I0025585

*Greetings, fellow traveler on this road of life!*

*Here, let me lend you my light until you get yours going again. I know! It's a bit blustery out here sometimes. No worries. I've been on this road a while, and I have some thoughts to help you on the way.*

*Who is this book for, you ask? Well, it's...*

*For young adults seeking unconditional love...*

*For those seeking the elusive instruction manual to parenting...*

*For those struggling with grief, addiction, mental health, burnout, or toxic relationships...*

*For those yearning for meaning, purpose, or reassurance that they are good enough and on the right path...*

*For anyone who simply needs to hear the words, "You are loved."*

***You are loved.***

*This book is for you.*

# The Lighthouse Guide

## Love & Advice from a Fellow Human

CHERI ALLAN

Five Oaks Books
2025

**The Lighthouse Guide**


Contact Information: cheri@cheriallan.com

Cover Image Credits:
Logo image © Elena Elisseeva | Dreamstime.com
Lighthouse Silhouette Vector Moonlight @ thailerderden10 | depositphotos.com
Glittering star dust circle @ tai11 | depositphotos.com

Interior Layout Image Credits:
Compass Rose #3 @ Volgarud | depositphotos.com
Water wave logo @ naseefahnada@gmail.com | depositphotos.com
Magic vector border w celestial stars @ Chorna_L | depositphotos.com



Publishing History
Five Oaks Books First Edition, 2025
Paperback ISBN: 978-0-9968955-3-8
Hardcover ISBN: 978-0-9968955-4-5
Digital ISBN: 978-0-9968955-2-1

Published in the United States of America

*To all the*
*torch-bearers,*
*light-seekers, and*
*wonder-filled wanderers.*

*May your collective light shine the way.*

# TABLE OF CONTENTS

(Should you wish to skip around. Go ahead. You make the rules!)

PART 7
## GRIEF



PART 8
## ADVERSITY & RESILIENCE

PART 9
## DECISION MAKING



PART 10
## FAITH, POLITICS, & THE GOLDEN RULE

PART 11
## WHO AM I?



PART 12
## WHY AM I HERE?



PART 13
## SOCIAL MEDIA

PART 14
## HOW TO BE HAPPY



PART 15
## THE GIFT OF GRATITUDE



PART 16
## JUST EXHALE

PART 17
## CONCLUDING THOUGHTS



## APPENDIX

PART 1

# INTRODUCTION

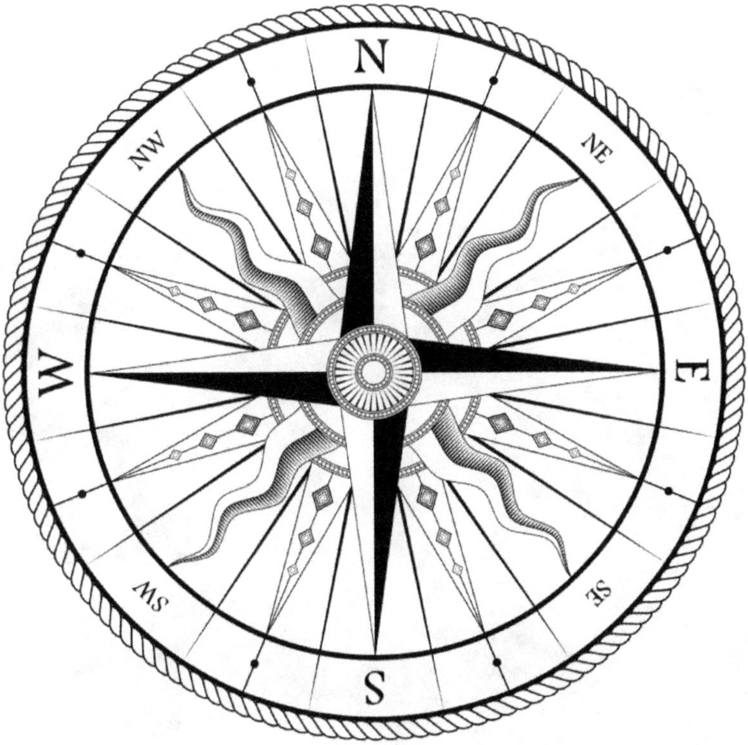

*Part 1: Introduction*

# MY LETTER TO YOU

Dear Reader,

As the saying goes, there are no new ideas, just new ways of expressing them. Before writing this book, I made the conscious decision not to read extensively on the subjects touched upon within it beyond verifying specific quotes or referenced ideas. This book was never intended as a definitive worldview or groundbreaking tome so much as this human's—my—thoughts as I've collected them like so many happy little stones in my pockets along this journey of life. I share them with you now. Some small and unassuming, some sparkling.

This book is no substitute for professional counseling or legal or financial advice. It is nothing more nor less than me sitting across from you at a metaphorical kitchen table, chatting about what is on your heart and me offering my piece. Feel free to read it from cover to cover or as whimsy, intuition, or the issue of the moment lead you. Take what resonates and leave what doesn't. I don't expect my thoughts to be universally applicable. They are just one perspective, hopefully a helpful one.

What this book is, is a love story. It's the story of how I, as I grew older, grew less cynical, more accepting, more open-minded. I fell more in love with humanity: beautiful, messy, quirky, complicated, big-feeling-ed humanity. And I want you to, too.

You deserve a world in which each of us brings our highest and best self to the journey before us. Where we live the golden rule in all we do.

I am like a lighthouse illuminating this limited shore of existence, hoping I can help those still navigating the stormy seas nearby to find comfort and hope, and know that, despite it all, they are not, and never will be, alone.

Peace and light, *Cheri*

# BEFORE WE BEGIN

This book is for you, of course, because all books are for the reader, but that made it very difficult to write. Who *are* you? Where are you on life's journey? What are your joys and sorrows, talents and flaws? With what are you struggling on this random day that ends in Y? These are questions I will never know the answers to, but I do know that something in me is drawn to sit with you in the space of this not-knowingness, to learn the questions on your heart, and to seek guidance to offer you.

Maybe your questions revolve around a relationship: a friendship, a romantic partner, a family member, or coworker. Maybe you are struggling with money and career: how to make it, when it's enough, how to save or spend wisely but generously. Perhaps you have lingering fears about more existential concerns: life and death, whether you are meant to have children, whether you are doing too much or not enough.

If so, I humbly offer this work.

Humbly being the operative word here, because—*hoo boy!*—it would be so easy for ego to take charge in a book offering advice, judgment too, but that's not what you're asking for, I'm guessing. So, instead, this guide is a series of stories, anecdotes, and related advice. It's sometimes brief and sometimes more involved and covers a variety of topics, so you can target an area of choice or read through at leisure. We are in this life together, existing as humans on this orbiting ball of amazement. If I have something to offer in experience or insight that you find helpful, it is yours.

That all said, why in the world should you even read this book or listen to *me*? Who am I to offer guidance or advice to anyone? This is a valid question, and I applaud you asking, because I think we should all be discerning about who we listen to in the age of mis and dis-information, don't you?

I am a mother. Although that is not all that defines me, it is one aspect everyone on earth will have familiarity with, so I begin there. I was a child of modest means in a household with two parents who loved one another, several siblings who intermittently fought but as adults do not. I went to college, earned my bachelor's degrees in Business and English, dated for several years before meeting my now husband (the Research Scientist). We went on to buy a small fixer-upper and have spent the last several decades renovating it, having two children, homeschooling them for a time (and then not), sending them off to college, watching them go on to advanced degrees, land their first jobs, travel, and fall in love in turn.

And through all that time, we have lived and loved and lost—pets, parents, jobs—but we've also traveled, hosted amazing parties, gotten very, very sick and somehow, miraculously, gotten better again. We lived through pandemic lockdowns and ice storms and familial dysfunction, and we've watched love bloom in those who thought their chances were over. My life has spanned the time of seeing the world embrace the internet and cell phones and technology and still have memories of canning food and splitting wood for the furnace.

This is to say, I am a human on this earth living in this time of great transition. So many people want to stop the clock and go back to "simpler" times when they were naïve of the struggles of those around them, even participated in adding to them, wittingly or not. They want to return to when they were ignorant of their own biases or self-centeredness. But no more than we can reverse the effects of climate change on our planet or erase the effects of time on our physical bodies, with the age of information, the naiveté of the past is gone. Burying one's head in the sand of time isn't an option, either—at least not a sustainable one. And as the wise and eloquent

Maya Angelou once said: "Do the best you can until you know better. Then when you know better, do better."

I want to do better.

Ideally, I would love to be in conversation with you, dear reader, because I'm excited about the possibilities for the future of this world we're in. I know there are a *lot* of people who dread change and actively run away from it. But if you are living this change in this moment and need a bit of the illumination of past experience to shine a light so you can navigate these seas of change safely and with more confidence, I'm here for you. You are welcome for tying that metaphor together, those of you who like predictability; I see you, too. Change is hard for you, so I will do my best to make this guide as simply and logically laid out as I can.

So, let's dig in. Make yourself a cup of tea or other warm something-something (coffee is my go-to, but if it's late, you know your body and what time you need to get up in the morning, make good choices), get yourself cozy, and sit with me for a bit.

We're in this thing called life together, and isn't that something to think about? (And if you heard The Artist Formerly Known as Prince singing just now, I see you, too.)

# Chapter 1

## YOU ARE LOVED

---

*In a perfect world you are loved unconditionally. In an imperfect world you are still loved unconditionally.*

---

My bedroom overlooks the forest outside our New England home, the branches of a youthful oak tree waving to me each morning. At night, my bedside light casts soft illumination, and I cannot count the times my now young adult children have come up and crawled under the thick down comforter or thrown themselves across the length and breadth of the bed just to talk.

I never feel so grateful as a parent as when I am sought out for comfort or advice or when my kids want to share something big or seemingly trivial that's happening to them in their lives or in the world, dreams they have forming, or ideas they want to test out in the space outside their brains. When we become one big pig pile of late-night chatting and someone decides to run for chips or tea, and then the cats or dogs come to be near, it's then that I know I *must* be doing something right. A lot of it isn't under my control, but the parts that are? They have an enormous impact.

I think the reason my kids seek me out even after my lights are off, is because they know without a doubt that the lights are always on *for them.* No matter the hour or what else I have going on, they have my unconditional love and undivided attention. Stuck on that paper? I'll read it for you. Unsure if this person is a good fit? Let's talk about why you feel that way.

Unconditional love means that no matter what they do or the choices they make, I will seek connection with them over judgment.

Seek connection over judgment.

This is like the age-old question for those in conflict: are you trying to resolve your argument or win it?

I may be a middle-aged mother easily dismissed, and there may well be countless more memorable people with more impressive credentials who could write a similar book, but they didn't. I did. I felt the call in a thousand small and profound ways to draw together the lessons I've learned in this lifetime in order to share them. As simple as they may seem, there are times that we don't trust our gut, we ignore the red flags, we believe (falsely) that the only one we can count on is ourselves, and in that disconnection and fierce, often trauma-induced independence, we isolate ourselves and cut ourselves off from the ties that give this life meaning.

There was no single reason I chose to write this book. It feels more like a case of this book demanding to be written—things The Universe in capital letters wanted me to pass along. There were plenty of times when I felt helpless to change the world for the better, and with hindsight many ideas which appear in this book are things I wish my younger self had known.

*Why do bad things happen to good people? Does everything happen for a reason? Why don't all parents love their children unconditionally and if their religion or social circle tells them to cast judgment instead of seeking connection, what will that do to their families and, by extension, the world?*

When I was younger and the AIDS epidemic was in full force and I would read about men—someone's brother or child—literally dying with no family to comfort them, I thought, "What parent would abandon their child like that? How is this love?"

This book was being written then even when I wasn't aware of it. It was being formed in my subconscious in response to the cruelty, uncertainty, the utter wrongness of so much of what I observed. If there were parents out there who couldn't or wouldn't love their child unconditionally, then I would be sure to parent my own children so that they *knew* they were loved.

This book was written back when I experienced unrelenting bullying, but also when I became the one who allowed the bullying. As I learned about the wrong ways to human and imagined the right ways, I made mistakes, but also grew.

I went off to college, met my now husband, got married, bought a house, and began a lifetime of hard-core DIY projects, including having children.

I'd seen my share of parenting fails, knew my parents loved me unconditionally, but like most parents, I still struggled to form a clear sense of what truly *good* parenting looked like. I knew it meant, at the very least, listening to your child and your gut. It meant not just providing for the physical body of a child but nurturing their mind and emotional health.

I had so many doubts and bumpy bits along the way, but when my eldest out of the blue left me a small handwritten note on my desk one day, I felt I'd won a parenting award. What did it say?

"Thank you for raising me to think critically instead of taking everything at face value."

Not only had I managed to safely bring this child to adulthood, I'd provided guidance for how to human.

But this book is about so much more than parenting.

This book is about navigating life's messiness while also dreaming of miracles. Over the years, we've had multiple medical crises rock our household, and even had addiction take hold of a loved one like it does for far too many. I've been a sounding board for friends going through divorce, losing spouses, and finding new love. I watched my kids fall in love for the first time, suffer heartbreak and move on to later, stronger partnerships.

Through it all, I questioned and doubted and wondered if the choices we were making were the right ones. Despite that doubt, there's one thing I know for certain: I am loved. So are you. In this crazy world of good things and rough times and big feelings, the one certainty is that *we are all loved.*

If you get nothing else from this book. If you stop here and walk away, I want you to know without any doubt that *you are loved.*

Maybe you aren't feeling that right now. That's okay. It's why this next chapter talks about loving and respecting yourself enough to know that you are worthy of love. You are meant to be here.

You deserve to *be.*

# Chapter 2
## TAKING UP SPACE

A few years ago, one of our kids brought a friend from college to our home for a visit. This was our first meeting, and while I knew a bit of this young woman's backstory, it told me nothing of her kind eyes and quiet, unassuming beauty. She had the sort of shy smile that transformed her features in a way that made you want to bring her joy just to see it again.

She was also terrified of dogs. In her home country, it is not uncommon for feral dogs to attack people, so despite our own dogs' desire to be her new best friend, it took a bit of coaxing to assure her our home was safe. She eventually made it past our entry and was introduced to domesticated cats for the first time. She became instantly enamored, and from that point on, explored our home with the wide eyes and the amazement of someone plunked on a distant planet and invited into the home of alien beings.

I did my best to engage in light conversation as we settled ourselves in the living room, asking her about how she came to be here, in my home, sitting on my couch, when her own country and family were thousands of miles away. I did my best, I say, because it was very obvious that despite all the hurdles she'd cleared to come to be sitting before me, she was very much a product of home: a country, family, and tradition that told women to be silent, small, and obedient.

It seemed obvious this young woman must be intelligent and courageous. She had to be! I mean, she was here pursuing a master's degree in a STEM field having secured grants to allow her the means to do so, and having travelled solo across the world to rental housing she'd secured.

I was eager to learn more, but after I again mentioned how amazing it was that she had come all this way to study and how smart she must be to have navigated that process entirely on her own, she demurred once again. Frustrated, I couldn't let it slide.

"You deserve to take up space," I said. "You have a voice. The Universe put you on this earth for a reason. You deserve to take up space and be heard."

I honestly will never know what prompted me to say these words in that moment. It was probably a bit more than either of us was prepared for. She turned away and brushed away the tears welling up in her eyes. Here I'd welcomed this woman into my home, terrified her with my dogs, and made her cry. Brilliant hosting.

"I mean it," I said, more gently. "I don't ever want you to make yourself smaller around me. Around any of us. In this house, you take up your rightful space, understood?"

She nodded. We moved on to petting the cats again.

But she heard me.

In the months that followed, she came to visit often, and our house became her home away from home. She marveled over the greens of spring outside our windows, joyfully pet the dogs she'd once been so afraid of, and greeted the cats before ever saying hello to the human occupants of the house. She graciously ate our American food and shared cuisine from her home country, went for walks through the woods with us, wished us well on special occasions from her own traditions, and shared in ours with interest and openness.

And through those months, the hunched and soft-spoken young woman we'd met that cold day in March began to stand taller, speak louder, share her thoughts and opinions, and wear brighter colors. I've watched her take up space, use her voice, and radiate curiosity and confidence. It's a work in progress as we all are, but the best reward is seeing, every time she walks through our door, her smile.

I adore that smile. That smile which transforms her features, comes from somewhere profound and beautiful and sacred. It's from a soul that has come to know that it was placed on this earth by The Universe for a reason.

---

*You deserve to take up space.*
*You deserve to be heard.*
*You were put on this earth for a reason.*

---

I believe all of those things with my whole heart and soul. I hope, by the end of this book, you will believe them, too. What's more, I hope you begin to move through your life speaking these things and sharing this view with those around you. Imagine, for a moment, if we *all* began to say and believe this about every person we met? Even those with whom we disagree or are in conflict with?

I see you balking, so I will put a caveat on this. No one deserves to take up *more* space than they afford their neighbor. No one deserves to speak more than they are willing to listen. Someone's reason for being here might be to learn how to be a better, more compassionate, more loving person. They might need to sit quietly and learn, but that is for them to discern and not to be imposed upon them.

Let's proceed, then, with the assumption that we are looking for universal truths, broad guidelines that will help us as individuals—but also as global citizens and communities—live more fulfilled, loving, equitable, joyful lives. There will always be exceptions and outliers. I cannot prove a negative, and this book isn't seeking to debate every anecdotal exception. If you, dear reader, struggle to hear my thoughts, then perhaps this book is not meant for you. I free you from sharing space with me or listening. I wish you well.

For all others, welcome! Don't mind the dogs. I look forward to getting to know you. I hope I can help illuminate the way for you as you navigate this thing called life. How amazing is it that we are here on this earth together? What a time to be alive?!

PART 2

# RELATIONSHIPS

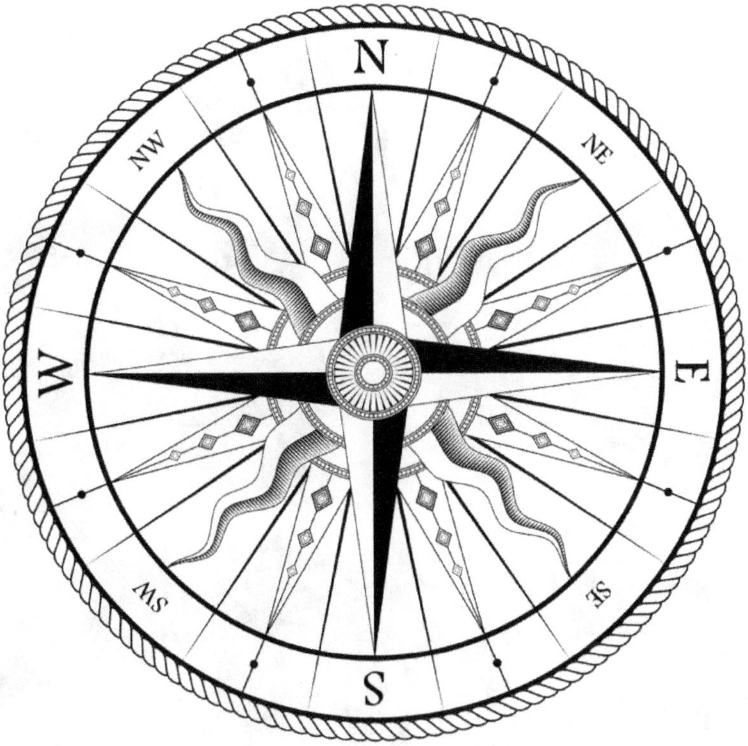

# Chapter 3

## RELATIONSHIPS

*You are loved.*
*You deserve to take up space.*
*You deserve to be heard.*

These are foundational truths to hold close when we consider what it means to be in relationship with others, because they are the foundation upon which we will judge healthy dynamics and set boundaries when needed. Too often we repeat unhealthy dynamics from our childhoods in adult relationships. The dynamics may be familiar, but they aren't always constructive to forming a strong sense of self-worth or loving reciprocity.

Repeat those truths above as often as needed until you *feel* them at your core. Build a solid foundation for yourself, know your worth, and you will be more able to form healthy relationships with others that nurture and support you.

## WHAT IS A HEALTHY RELATIONSHIP?

I like to think of a healthy relationship as a two-way street. A healthy relationship is an active and mutual pursuit, never a prize nor a possession. We don't *have* a relationship so much as are *in* one. A healthy relationship requires give and take and mutual respect. We all know that depleted feeling of being the giver to a taker. That sort of parasitic existence, while a form of relationship, is never described as a healthy one, because one party is exhausted in favor of the other.

In this chapter, I hope to explore all the many and varied forms of relationship, with one's self, friends, a higher power, strangers, romantic partners and from there we can think about what makes each of these *healthy* relationships, what red flags are, and how to navigate dysfunction (because we live in the real world).

## RELATIONSHIP WITH SELF

### A Lesson in Forgiveness

I once led a youth discussion group in our congregation. At the time, there were a series of rather public incidents with well-known individuals who had photos from the past where they had engaged in questionable behavior. As these photos came to light, they were followed by calls for these individuals to step down from prominent positions in office or to be "cancelled" as artists. It made me wonder if there is ever room to forgive past behavior but also for individuals (even adults) to grow and learn, the chance to, as Mayou Angelou says, "do better." Or, are we given one shot at living perfect lives?

I asked this group of teens to take a moment and reflect on something they had either done or said at any point in their lives for which they were ashamed—to recall an incident where they behaved their very worst. I asked them to really think about those impacted by their words or actions and how those negatively impacted must have felt.

I looked at each face around me as they recalled that moment, their personal low point. I watched as shoulders hunched and eyes darted around the group as if we could see into each other's memories. I knew they were thinking that soon they would be asked to reveal their own worst behavior.

But that's not what I did next.

I said, "Now imagine that from now on, and throughout the rest of our lives, we will be judged on and known for our own worst moment. It will be the moment that defines who we are and how others perceive us.

"It doesn't feel good, does it? That sense that there is no room for personal growth, no space for forgiveness?"

In that exercise, it was all too easy for each of us to remember a moment in our past for which we were ashamed. Forty years later, I can still recall the face of a girl sitting in the school library whose social awkwardness had made her a target for bullying—where I had the choice to speak up but chose to remain silent. I remember the comments I've made over the years that while not intended to be cruel, lacked tact or sensitivity, and for which I was too embarrassed in the moment to apologize. I remember the times I chose my own comfort over another's dignity.

It's human to behave badly, selfishly, even cowardly. In reflecting on those moments, though, we have the capacity to forgive our younger, fallible selves, and to grow into better people. When we show compassion and grace for those who have committed wrongs, we practice forgiveness but also hold space for forgiving ourselves. (See Chapter 6 for more on the topic of forgiveness.)

It's often said that people are their own worst enemies, and after this exercise with the teens, I could see how it would be all too easy to fixate on that one moment of poor judgment, cruelty, or self-centeredness and self-flagellate from that point forward. If the exercise above brought up an unwelcome memory from your past, it might well affect how you are feeling about yourself right this moment.

I invite you to sit with that for a moment.

Now imagine yourself making amends in whatever way is possible such that you are able to afford yourself forgiveness. Knowing that we are all prone to making mistakes and, hopefully, learning from them, I invite you to now sit in a space of self-forgiveness and grace.

A healthy relationship with self goes beyond forgiving yourself for having not behaved up to your own ideals, sometimes it is about rejecting the limiting views of those around us. If anyone or any institution tells you that you have to make yourself smaller, quieter, less *you* in order to be acceptable, know that those words and norms are about control and not making you better. More specifically, those norms are about retaining control or wresting it from you. It's only the norm if you play along and accept it. Don't.

Another way to foster healthy relationship with self is through trust—trusting your own gut, intuition, spide-y senses, or "knowing". Trust your own feelings, observations, and memories. Too often others use fear or gaslighting to make us discount our own perceptions and sense of reality. Trust in self builds self-esteem and courage. It provides for a stable foundation from which to raise any necessary boundaries and from which to build bridges of genuine connection.

Finally, and probably most importantly, hear these words (again): you are loved. The universe conspired to bring you into existence, to breathe life into you, and to gift you this human experience. It is a messy, unpredictable existence, a fleeting moment in cosmic history, so don't you dare waste a nanosecond of it internalizing harsh messaging from the outside world. Know your worth. *Know* it, *show* it, and *live* it. No matter what is happening, feel that breath in your lungs and tell yourself: what a time to be alive!

## LOVING WHO YOU ARE

It's not an easy road to live this life in a body that others may deem the wrong size, color, shape, or kind, to know that the way we think or act or express interest or love is too [something] to be "acceptable." And all I want to say is: that's bullshit. I'm sorry to offend, but if you're offended by my righteous outrage about some members of humanity policing other members of humanity for things that don't affect anyone else, then you deserve to hear me swear.

For everyone else: I see you, I celebrate you, I want you to be the you that you feel called to be. Get the haircut, the body art, the piercings, wear the clothes, say the words, sing the songs, dance the dances, love the people and be the *you*-est you imaginable. Because, at the end of this brief nanosecond of existence, you will have wanted to have found your vibe, your tribe, and your jam before time ran out.

## SETTING PERSONAL BOUNDARIES

Fun fact: In my early thirties, I was the sole breadwinner for our household as my husband was a stay-at-home father to our two-year-old, I'd just had a miscarriage, was working a highly demanding job… and I nearly died from sepsis. (I promise this has a happy ending but more on that later.)

To this day I don't have clarity on what landed me in the hospital for four precarious days, curled into a ball in my hospital bed hitting the time-dosed dispenser for my morphine drip like I was trying to reach high score on a video game.

All I know is that eventually I was deemed well enough to be sent home, weak, exhausted, still in pain, and feeling more mortal and vulnerable than at any other time in my life.

Sudden, severe illness or accidents can profoundly change a person. For me the lessons were two-pronged: I couldn't do "it" alone—life, parenting, you name it—and, two, there was power in being able to say "no."

Before falling sick, I not only felt that I was invincible but also that I *had* to be. From providing a home and income for our family, to being a mother, to being a daughter to my widowed mom, I was stretching myself thin in every direction. But the truth was I *wanted* to do all those things. Being a mother was something I'd waited eight years to become after getting married. I wanted to continue working on our fixer-upper house making it the home I dreamed of. I felt an obligation to be present for my mother who'd lost her partner in life long before anyone thought would happen. It was a struggle to say, "no" to invitations to become involved in work or events or fundraisers that I wanted so much to support.

But, after emerging from that hospital so many years ago, I knew I needed to learn how to say "no" to the endless requests on my time and energy.

In truth I only needed to learn how to say, "Not yet."

"Not yet" gives space to consider whether an invitation is one we want to act on or revise.

"Not yet" leaves room for all the things we want to do when the time is right.

"Not yet" doesn't close the door but leaves it ajar. It is the key to setting a mental health and life-saving personal boundary.

This small phrase allows us room to breathe, a time-out from the demands of those around us, and there is no shame in that.

Check in with yourself often. "Not yet" allows space to do so.

## FRIENDSHIPS

*"People come into your life for a reason, a season, or a lifetime."* ~ Brian A. Chalker

I've experienced it as an adult and watched my kids experience it as they grew. We all have had friends who have come into our lives and then, for whatever reason, have moved out of our lives again. That passage can be particularly painful, because the loss often feels like a personal rejection.

In looking back to those friendships that didn't last, I can see that they were often formed because of proximity or a shared experience and less on a common value system or spiritual connection. If that friend moves or goes off to college, or that experience that brought us together evolves, sometimes those friendships dissolve. I like to think of those cases as two main characters living their own stories whose plots diverge. No harm, no foul. They were friendships for a season. The individual, rich stories of our lives continue in our own series. Godspeed.

Sometimes a friend comes into our life because we or they need to learn something. Maybe we (or they) are replaying some dysfunctional pattern from childhood that needs to be worked through as an adult. Perhaps we need to learn discernment, how to stand up for ourselves, or how to be in connection without feeling drained from always being the "giver". Those are friendships for a reason. They are meant to show us our worth and the expectations we should have for the privilege of being in our lives. Usually, thankfully, they dissolve when the lesson is learned.

A friendship for a lifetime is something different and profound. These connections are able to withstand distance and silence and evolving personal lives. Those rare and wondrous friendships weather periods of busyness that take us away from one another without missing a beat. They rest comfortably on shared humor, heartfelt honesty, and often have a "survived the war in the trenches together" quality to them.

Nurture those friendships. Make time for them. These are the friendships that help us navigate life's heartaches and the friends who eagerly celebrate every success. These are the friends that know the real, unvarnished versions of us and still want the very best for us. We leave interactions with them feeling uplifted and hopeful. If we don't, that's something to be examined.

There is no such thing as a single *best* friend especially as one ages. We can and should have multiple friends with whom we share deep connection, and true friends will want that for us. They will know that they will not always be able to be the solution to the problems in our life, nor will they always have the bandwidth.

Find and nurture relationships with those special people who whoop with joy over your successes and special moments, sit with you overnight in the ER when you are sick and scared, who bring you food to eat and hugs without words when you are grieving, and who will add colorful punctuation to every venting session. Your close friends are the family you would have chosen had you been given the choice, and to be that someone for someone else? It's the highest honor there is.

## RELATIONSHIP WITH GOD, CREATION, AND OTHER BIG THINGS

I was raised in the Catholic Church. I remember the stern-faced nuns in catechism class who reprimanded the children practicing for First Communion who dared turn their heads to look behind them.

I remember the deacon who handed out the bulletins at the entry each week with a kind smile.

Mostly, I remember how numb my bottom would become each Sunday as I watched with equal parts boredom and fascination as the priest mumbled in Latin and performed the rituals leading to Communion.

Even seven-year-old me had thoughts about my faith. Where were the women? Why did they all seem so unhappy? Why could I not speak directly to God? Did "he" not understand a seven-year-old girl? Was "he" even a "he"? And if there was only One God, why did we break him into pieces for the Holy Trinity? So many questions.

In college, I took a class in which I learned for the first time the history surrounding the Protestant Reformation led by Martin Luther, and I began to reflect more deeply on the religious traditions and dogma I'd been raised to follow without question.

As my now husband and I planned our wedding, we chose not to marry in the Catholic Church. His very traditional family wasn't pleased, but my own mother who had converted to Catholicism to marry my father had this to say: "I'm just glad that you are being married in a church."

For her, it was more important for me to have a relationship with God than to follow any specific tradition, and I've held that foremost in my heart ever since. It is the loving intention behind the traditions that matters most to me, not the traditions or even any specific faith tradition itself.

Over the years, I've exchanged both Christmas and Hannukah gifts with friends, celebrated a Bar Mitzvah, attended weddings from a variety of faith traditions, and generally observed how people and their faith practices impact their lives.

The more I've learned about the many religious teachings and practices from around the world, the more convinced I am there is no right way to be a moral or faith-based human. Humans are by nature a creation of the divine, their variety a testament to the vast beauty inherent in the universe.

That's not to say that all religious teachings and traditions are divine. I think most of us have seen the less desirable rigid control, overreach, and unfortunate corruption within organized religion around the globe, where stringent behavioral teachings are less about morality or spiritual growth than about filling the coffers or making sure the flock is fearful enough not to stray from obedient control.

(I gently apologize if you are shocked by my words, but I also stand by them.)

One of the reasons I moved away from the faith of my childhood is because I have strong reservations about any religious practice which tells believers what to think without also granting the freedom to question and discuss those beliefs. It is not a true faith if we have not been challenged and chosen to remain committed. Blind faith is simple obedience. Neither does such obedience serve the believer, because it hasn't been tested.

Too often people find themselves in a crisis of faith when their obedience is not met with the results they are made to expect. Their prayers are not answered. Their public displays of piety not rewarded.

A faith born from personal connection with Source can be enhanced and celebrated in more traditional religious practice, but without having gone through the work of forming that relationship with our Higher Power, it will frequently fail to support us when our lives, inevitably, challenge us.

Beyond this, any faith which seeks to dictate who and how I can express love to other humans, which seeks to exclude others or isolate believers, which preaches superiority instead of inclusion, or enriches itself over choosing to share the bounty of this existence, is not about building relationship with Spirit or God. That's about the institution, earthly and human-defined hierarchies, and preservation of control and power. I said what I said.

I enthusiastically co-sign any faith practice which encourages direct and authentic relationship with Spirit, knowing that the expression of this sacred relationship is as varied and beautiful as the inhabitants of this earth.

If ever I am in doubt, I simply ask myself: where is the love? Therein lies my moral compass, my north star. Love.

## SHARING WITH STRANGERS

While we're semi on the topic of religion… It's a bit funny to me that so many Christians read the parable of the loaves and fishes and say to themselves, "Jesus works miracles!" Which, sure, that's certainly a valid take, but I see something more relevant to the rest of us humans in that story, beyond an all-powerful deity at work. You see (in case you aren't familiar with it), in the Gospel of Matthew is the story where Jesus went outside the city to the desert with his disciples to preach, and there, thousands of people gathered to listen. The people grew hungry, and when Jesus asked for the disciples to collect the food available to share with the crowd all they came up with were five loaves of bread and two fishes, hardly enough for thousands of hungry bellies. Well, Jesus raised them up, blessed the bread and fish, and instructed his disciples to begin passing out the food.

Everyone ate their fill, and when the disciples gathered the leftovers, there were, miraculously, twelve baskets of food remaining.

Now there are scholars who can speak to the twelve tribes of Israel and other symbolism, but whenever I heard this parable taught it was used as a lesson wherein: "with Jesus, all things are possible!" And also, "Jesus works miracles!"

Maybe. That is certainly a take I've heard countless times over the years. But what if we pause and consider this story as a lesson in abundance?

I see it as a lesson in community. When I read this story, I see Jesus as demonstrating that when we *all* share what we have, *there will be enough.*

Are you to tell me that women and children and families trekked out to listen to Jesus in the desert and not one person thought to pack a snack? Please. You and I both know that there would have been the equivalent of granola bars, apples, and water bottles tucked into pockets and wrapped in cloth pouches. Jesus set the example that sharing, however small our contribution might seem, when combined with everyone else's part will always be more than enough for all.

His lesson was less about how powerful or blessed *he* was and more about learning to see the world as being a place of abundance and not scarcity.

Be generous.

Trust in abundance.

Remember the story *Stone Soup*? Same exact lesson.

# Chapter 4

## NAVIGATING THE TRICKY BITS

### A FRESH START, WITH CONDITIONS

---

> *"I cannot forget the follies and vices of others so soon as I ought, nor their offences against myself... My good opinion once lost is lost forever."* ~ Fitzwilliam Darcy, *Pride & Prejudice*

---

I've noticed that most people fall into two camps when it comes to setting boundaries: the first are those quick to forgive even if it means opening themselves up to hurt again. The second camp are the Mr. Darcys of the world. Once burned, forever shy. So, is it possible to forgive and forget and continue a relationship after betrayal or breach of trust? Yes, and no.

Yes, I think we can, with effort, identify the manner in which the other person let us down or harmed us, but then the work of setting boundaries for future interactions is, well, *work.* The onus is on us, the harmed, to decide the rules of engagement for future interaction. Gone is the open and free vulnerability that makes healthy relationships easy. And that's where I see any further relationship as less of a true relationship—where two or more are giving and taking in equal measure—because when boundaries must be set, one side is already engaged in metering and monitoring those exchanges.

Setting boundaries is a way of reducing or mitigating future harm if contact must be preserved, but it will be very difficult to move back to a space of trust and openness without a great deal of intentional work and honest communication.

One form of boundary setting is termed "gray rocking" where we disengage from an emotional response to another's behavior. It is in a similar vein as the "Let Them" approach which I encourage you to explore if either of these feel appropriate to your situation. The bottom line is that when we are in emotionally abusive or dysfunctional relationships and must maintain contact, minimizing our emotional reactions or distancing ourselves from the offender can be strategies to help remove our reaction—a reward which narcissistic or manipulative personalities often seek. However, limiting our emotional engagement can take a toll, and the very real risk of disassociating entirely may make us feel less emotionally alive than we'd prefer. In all cases, I encourage finding a trusted and skilled counselor to work through any specific situation.

My mother-in-law was a difficult and flawed human. I will try not to share too much, as I hope she finds the light and compassion (wherever her soul now resides) she was so unwilling to share whilst on this earth. It was abundantly clear from our very earliest interactions that those around her walked on eggshells. I didn't understand the nature of the dysfunction tied to her until decades later, but I think it boiled down to a mindset of scarcity versus abundance. If someone near was happy, she professed how miserable she was. If she had given of her time or attention, she expected she was therefore owed the same or more. Her relationships were transactional and any love she professed to give was conditional.

It is difficult to be in open and vulnerable relationship with such a person, and it was harder still to institute boundaries that felt enough for those of us in her orbit but didn't strike her as our withholding what was justly hers.

Going "no contact" didn't feel like a workable option given her health needs, lack of mobility, and our sense of obligation as family. In hindsight, I see that the "bond of family" was used as a tool of manipulation. She was fond of using phrases such as "blood is thicker than water," "family is everything", "you are your brother's keeper," etc. But, these myths, or reductionist views of much more complex ideas, were harmful and used as tools to manipulate us into remaining in unhealthy relationship.

## REFRAMING THE MYTHS THAT HARM US

How many of us have been twisted into toeing the line with family because "blood is thicker than water" or guilted into some sacrifice or oversight because "you are your brother's keeper"? These oft-quoted lines are inevitably used to guilt us into behavior we feel isn't serving our best interests because... *family.*

Well, I'm here to tell you that it's time to reframe these harmful myths or at least explore their full context. For instance, I've recently heard a more complete quote and that is:

---

*The blood of the covenant is thicker than the water of the womb.*

---

This is to say that chosen bonds and found family, are matters of free will, and because we *choose* them, they are more meaningful and powerful bonds than the happenstance of a family you might somehow be born into. If you look into the history of the quote and its many derivations, there is clearly a pattern of those who choose to truncate the passage in Deuteronomy 33:9 to "blood is thicker than water" in order to imply that blood relations are a bond stronger than anything else. Conversely, there are the more nuanced versions which suggest that blood is thicker than a mother's milk (meaning a vow is stronger than those who might have been nursed at the same breast.)

For many of us, however, we intuitively know that shared experience or understanding and even pain (blood) can forge a stronger connection than any genetic tie. Anyone who insists that a person should prioritize familial ties to the exclusion of others is likely doing so because they don't want to put in the effort to qualify as chosen family. Yes, I said it.

We should all strive to be chosen family regardless of genetic connections.

That all said, I have been in situations where I've been hurt deeply and profoundly. Anyone who has been impacted by addictions, infidelity, or financial irresponsibility, or any number of other situations understands. When someone we are in relationship with lies to us, trust is broken. I made the decision to allow this individual a second chance, but my guard was most definitely up. This individual had to make real amends, but also, *I* had to do the internal work of seeing how I had contributed to what had happened either directly or by not becoming more involved when red flag behaviors initially presented themselves. I had to have tough conversations not only with this individual but with myself. It was only in the space of that absolute vulnerability—the breaking down of the previous relationship to its very foundation—that we were able to rebuild anew from a place of honest communication and understanding. In this instance, we were able to successfully rebuild with guardrails in place, but unlike toxic relationships where one party sets a boundary, in this case we agreed on guardrails to help us both scaffold our connection until it was strong enough to trust in again.

## SEPARATING FROM TOXICITY: GOING NO CONTACT

I married into a family that had a long history of dysfunctional and toxic behavior. This is a truth I share not to shame but to shed light. Those who were involved are free to share their truth. Those for whom this is new information I absolve of culpability.

I first met my husband when I was nineteen. I'd been raised in a loving household with two parents who cared for me to the best of their ability. They modeled love and support. This was not my future husband's experience.

We spent decades jumping through imaginary hoops, striving to clear ever-moving goalposts, and walking on eggshells. If you name a narcissistic behavior, we lived through it. It was years after the individual in question passed before we began to unpack all that we'd experienced and how it had affected our sense of emotional safety, ability to name and express big feelings, and our confidence in our own reality. (Hello, gaslighting!)

So, when we recognized toxic behaviors in another family member and its effects on us, we made the difficult decision to go no contact.

For anyone who has chosen to break off familial ties, you understand how fraught this decision can be. I offer some thoughts on how we navigated this decision and how it helped us be at peace with it.

**Make a conscious choice.** First, we openly discussed the decision and the reasons behind it with each other (spouse to spouse), with a therapist, and with our minister. These conversations were essential to validating our perception that the behavior we believed we were witnessing was a.) indeed happening, b.) not healthy for us, and c.) we were choosing an ethical and moral path forward. More on this later. A supportive friend or family member not directly involved in the situation might also prove helpful, but be careful to avoid consulting those whose personal experience or closeness to the situation may color how they show up for you in this moment, as their own trauma may make them want to live vicariously through you or their lack of objectivity may cause them to sympathize with maintaining an unhealthy status quo.

**Document the decision.** I chose to write an email to the individual explaining that going no contact was a decision we had made, that it was due to behavior we found wasn't healthy for us to be around, and that we had observed that due to past trauma interactions only tended to trigger both parties. I encouraged the recipient to seek out their own healing journey, expressed gratitude they had individuals they could lean on for emotional support, but that there was no hope for reconciliation with us, and that they should not attempt to contact us nor would we be contacting them.

**Block and set boundaries.** One of the a-ha moments we had was that the family member in question had used text messages and other platforms as direct access to deliver toxicity. Because we didn't have those communication channels locked down, we were unwittingly participating in our own victimization. We blocked this individual on social media, their aliases, their phone number, and so the only points of contact were if they chose to drive the distance to our house or use email.

**Reinforce the boundary when breached.** (They will always try.) When the recipient inevitably attempted to seek contact (through email) I was perfunctory in replying where it was necessary to impart information I felt they were due, respectfully declined to update them on the family (no news is good news!), and eventually allowed future emails to go unanswered. I allowed this easing away over the period of months, because for me and our situation it felt both kinder to the person involved as it trained them that our boundary was firm and it trained *me* in how to compassionately but firmly maintain the boundary we'd set.

I specifically made the decision to send an email with our decision, because it helped me state my case in a space where I could choose my words carefully, express all I felt the need to express, but also to formally set a boundary.

Too often, we avoid or ghost people in our lives when circumstances get awkward, and in some situations, that is the absolute right thing to do. In this instance, it felt right to compassionately identify specific behaviors they might reflect upon before making it clear we were setting our own healthy boundary going forward. In this way, I felt I'd done what I could to encourage them on a path of growth or self-awareness should they choose to take it while also making it clear that that journey for their own healing could and would not involve us.

I'm well aware that there are situations where safety is an issue or where someone can't, for their own mental health, have any contact. This is why I stepped in as the person communicating the decision we made as a family, because I felt least emotionally impacted by this individual and so any contact would be less fraught for me.

The decision to go no contact wasn't an easy one until it was made, and then it's a decision we wish we had made years before. Our clergy person was very helpful in helping us see our decision as not only morally acceptable (God wouldn't ask you to sacrifice yourself for another) but also pointed out that if we believe we are each put on this earth to learn something and grow spiritually

(YMMV) then by remaining in a toxic relationship without asking the other party to show respect for us, we are depriving them of the impetus or opportunity to grow as an individual. Setting a boundary no matter whether it is no contact or some other limit on interactions is insisting that another treat us and our loved ones with a minimum amount of respect and love, and, honestly, if someone isn't willing to hear our needs and work to meet them, how are either of us benefiting from that relationship?

Sometimes setting a boundary is us telling another we care enough to want to see them grow and they can't do that while we are allowing them to be dependent on us in unhealthy ways.

---

*Boundaries empower us. They are a predetermined response to another's behavior.*

---

Boundaries are for us to know how we will respond to another's actions. It is not up to *them* to respect our boundaries as much as it is up to *us* to define and enforce them. Boundaries do not demand another change their behavior. Rather, a boundary is us insisting that certain conditions be met for another to be in contact with us. When I think about it, we do this all the time as we navigate the world. We expect a base level of decorum and civility from strangers on the street. It makes perfect sense that we would have *at least* this level of expectation from someone with whom we choose to interact with and be vulnerable with on any regular basis.

## HOLIDAYS, CELEBRATIONS, AND THE WEIGHT OF EXPECTATIONS

We don't live in a perfect world, though, and not every relationship is one that we have either the outside support to change or the internal bandwidth to reject or rebuild. Sometimes, an unpleasant connection just *is*.

I survived decades of holidays crushed under the expectations of a toxic mother-in-law. Never satisfied with anything from food to gifts to the weather, this woman was the most water-logged of wet blankets imaginable. I realize now, though, that expectations? They are our enemy. An expectation is anticipated resentment and disappointment. Let me say that again:

---

*An expectation is anticipated resentment.*

---

Every expectation is us opening ourselves to the inevitable monkey wrench that will leave us unhappy, unsatisfied, and unfulfilled. An expectation limits us to preconceived notions of delight or despair and prohibits us from experiencing what may unfold.

If we don't expect to have food we'll enjoy, we have the choice to make a suggestion or bring our own.

If we don't think anyone will give us a gift we'd like, we have the choice to offer gift ideas or suggest we each buy ourselves a gift to open together, or even plan a "no gifts" gathering.

If we don't like the time others have planned to gather, we have the choice of arriving late, leaving early, or opting out altogether.

If we don't want to partake in a tradition, a prayer, the consumption of any food or drink we find offensive or unpleasant, we can choose to opt out without passing judgment on those who choose to partake.

If our expectation of participation is that we will not enjoy attendance, we can choose to stay home or partake in an alternative activity.

We can choose to be open to: surprise gifts given with good intention, new foods, new traditions, a change in schedule, a change in seating arrangements, weather interference, or suggestions of the moment for a game, a walk, or a new idea.

My most beloved holidays were those in which the weather stranded us alone as a family, where my mother slept over on the couch when the kids were little just to enjoy a holiday morning with them before going off to other family, where we were introduced to traditions from another culture which we joyfully integrated into our holiday, or where we tried to adapt to a preferred cuisine and sadly, and hilariously, failed to meet the mark. (My sincerest apologies for the inedible vegetarian loaf. I did try!)

Expectations in life, but particularly when attached to holidays and celebrations, can inhibit our ability to roll with life's unpredictability.

Allow space for life to intervene, for whimsy to take root, for traditions to evolve with changing times and influences. You will be richer for it.

# Chapter 5

## ROMANCE, MARRIAGE, AND OTHER COMMITMENTS

Now that I've completely turned you off to the idea of joining your known dysfunction with the unknown quirks of another's family, it seems the perfect time to talk about finding that special someone. I suppose now that you've been fortified with talk about how it can all go wrong, I'm here to share that sometimes it can all go wonderfully right.

### DATING

This sub-chapter could very well be an entire book, but you didn't pick up this book to learn about dating, so I'll keep things brief.

First, I'm going to say it: if someone is below twenty, there should be no more than a one or two-year age gap for a romantic relationship. Yes, I said it. By one's early twenties, that age gap can span up to two to four years without triggering awkward pop-culture-reference confusion between partners or real-life power imbalances. Once we've reached our upper twenties, our prefrontal cortex is fully-formed, we've finished our education, we likely live independently, we've gotten our first car or pet and are in a career. At this point, we are an adult who can make our own decisions.

Carry on.

I say this because too often we allow teens too young to make life-altering decisions to become involved with those who have the means to exert control in unhealthy ways. This is grooming, not romance, and shame on those who don't protect young adults and teens from abuse.

Let's assume, then, that we're not talking about predatory behavior but about a real desire for healthy romantic connection.

Dating should be fun. I know it's often very much not, but fun should be the goal, no matter our age. Daters are, ostensibly, looking for a partner to share life with—shouldn't that be enjoyable? So, I encourage everyone to meet people organically vs. online, because then we're more likely to be meeting them in an environment that we frequent and perhaps doing something we both enjoy. We shouldn't discount online dating but I wouldn't recommend relying on it.

I've not personally experienced dating via dating apps, so you are free to ignore that follows, but as an observer, it seems prudent to speak directly with someone new either via video or (preferably) in-person as soon after you begin to chat as possible. Extended messaging keeps the connection living in a digital landscape of not-quite-reality when you want to make a real-world connection. Many a cat-fisher has used the cover of digital spaces to their advantage. Just saying.

When you do decide to meet, start small. Do not commit to dinner or a long hike or anything bigger than a brief coffee, drink, or lunch-time stroll in a public park. If things are going to progress, you will both make time and space for more. If they are not, you can bow out gracefully without having to suffer through a meal with a less-than-desirable companion.

But honestly, please, no ghosting. Rejection is hard. It is made harder when it's vague or opaque or cruel. Pay your way until one or the other of you decides you want to treat the other. If this person isn't for you, you can engage in a conversation as long as it takes to finish your iced coffee and say, "It was lovely to meet you. I'm sorry we don't feel more of a connection. I wish you the best."

If it's easier to do the rejecting via text once you are no longer face-to-face, that's okay, but please be clear but kind, be honest but firm, then move on.

That said, follow your yeses but also your maybes. Don't be too quick to rule someone out as a romantic interest unless you have obvious red flags or "I feel like I'd have more fun cleaning the bathroom" interest. The friendship-vibes? Be honest that it's not feeling romantic, but maybe follow that a bit further down the road. Many lasting partnerships began as friendships and blossomed. When we dismiss someone too early in a relationship it can be because we're following old, unhealthy patterns. We may feel like the peace and safety we feel with a potential healthy match isn't "exciting" enough, and there's danger in that. Because, yes, everyone wants to be eager to see their new crush, but we sometimes misinterpret what our physiology is telling us.

It's easy to mistake anxiety or conflict for chemistry. Both raise our pulse rate, but only chemistry has the potential for a healthy relationship long-term. That said, don't mistake physical chemistry for compatibility. Chemistry has to do with getting along when the lights are off. Compatibility is about getting along when the lights are on, as well.

Listen to your intuition about whether someone is safe or kind to be around. The gut always seems to know, doesn't it? Make an effort not to ignore red flags just because the person is hot (or wealthy, or any number of superficial reasons.) I'll probably say it again, but it's so important in those early days to pay attention to how you *feel* when you are leaving this person after spending time together. Is it relief? Is it insecurity? If so, those are red flags.

If things are going well, though, try to arrange a meet-up with their friends and family as soon as is reasonable. A sign that they are considering you for a longer-term connection is introducing you to their extended social sphere of friends, family or coworkers. It's a red flag if you've been dating for weeks and haven't met anyone. Nobody wants to be a side piece, the "other woman", or any other less-than-up-front situationship that won't lead to the partnership most of us are looking for.

Now about intimacy. I know there are lots of "rules" about how soon people recommend physical intimacy, and all I will say is: do whatever works for you. Every romantic connection arrives at physical intimacy at a unique pace, and the only people to determine the best timing and the amount of intimacy are those involved. Period. You will know it's the right timing for you and your partner when both of you are giving enthusiastic consent for whatever you engage in. Consent isn't a barely-perceptible nod or muffled "yes" or "sure". It is, "YES, PLEASE!!!!" This is your green light.

Check in with your partner(s) early and often about how they are feeling, listen, and accept that consent is given *until it is retracted* and that can be *at any point, for any reason.* No one is owed intimacy. Expecting it in return for doing nice things or providing a meal is manipulation and prostitution not to mention a huge red flag. (In fact, it is grossly transactional, and if you feel this way, please seek counseling.)

Find someone who will move at your most comfortable pace, use your voice to express both your consent and your boundaries, and know that the person who will care for you long-term is the person who listens, respects your boundaries, and makes you feel safe to be your most vulnerable.

Beware workplace romances. I know, it's where many of us spend most of our waking hours, but workplace romances are rife with the risks of power imbalances, potential conflicts of interest, can negatively affect your or your coworker's comfort especially if things go sideways, and are definitely a "tread lightly" and "have an exit plan" situation in my book. Out of office or work conference flings are rooted in secrecy and the excitement of taboo and are least likely to pan out well for anyone. If you are determined to pursue an office romance, move slowly and intentionally and only after getting to know this person very well on a friendship basis first. I wouldn't proceed unless you are ready to tell Human Resources about it and are prepared for any negative consequences.

For every romance, once you are seeing one another more frequently, take selfies and other pictures of your special someone. If this relationship grows, you will love to look back on your early days together. And if it sours? You have something to delete or make memes out of. Win-win either way.

One final note in a section where we are talking about looking for love: love often happens when we decide we are done looking or not actively looking. We've heard it a thousand times: happy couples report that love came to them when they least expected it or had "stopped" dating. It happened to me!

I had made the conscious decision to focus on my studies and step off the emotional roller-coaster of dating and then, literally, two months later, I started spending time with my now husband. Why is this experience so common? I have a few thoughts.

One, we are done pretending to be someone we are not. We're no longer anxiously trying to make ourselves more attractive, more entertaining, more seductive, and so our authentic nature shines through.

Two, we become less anxious and needy. Our vibe is chill.

Three, we aren't placing ourselves in situations where those who trawl for quick hook-ups tend to congregate. Instead, we are in our normal lives, doing the activities we love, so we are more likely to self-select like-minded and aligned people and to delight them with our natural enthusiasm for the things we're passionate about.

Not "looking" for love means we've also taken the pressure off of a budding friendship to become something more before it's ready.

So, if you're "done" with dating and just want to live life? Do it! Be open to the possibility of connection with new people, and love may well follow when you least expect it.

## RED FLAGS

I won't lie to you. Dating can be a minefield, especially if we haven't taken the time to reflect on our own insecurities or traumas. It's painfully easy to groundhog-day our way through partner after partner without realizing that the common denominator is ourself. I'm not calling anyone out, because this is human nature and often a part of the process of learning what we do want in that special someone. But, sometimes, the failure of a relationship really does lie in the other person. So, as a help, I've assembled a non-exhaustive list of red flags—reasons you might want to think twice about entering into a relationship with or remaining in relationship with someone.

In no particular order:

**You've already broken up.** This may seem an odd place to start for red flags, but over the years I've often observed couples break up, make up, and break up again, in an endless cycle of hopefulness and angst, so my first bit of relationship wisdom is this:

---

*If you break up, it's for a reason.*

---

I'm just going to say it: those couples who get to the point of breaking up almost never succeed long-term. I know. I know! There are exceptions! (There are always exceptions.) But what I have seen is that those couples who break up usually do so for one of four reasons which are difficult to overcome:

1. a breach of trust (e.g. infidelity, lying about an addictive behavior, finances, and the like),

2. a mismatch in communication styles or poor communication in general ("you never listen" or "you don't understand"),

3. a mismatch in goals, lifestyle, or values (party animal dating the introvert, free spirit dating the type-A workaholic), or worst of all,

4. contempt for or indifference to the other party. (This is a death knell. If your partner doesn't seem to care about you, your welfare, or your happiness, it's over. There's no coming back from this. Please move on with your best life.)

Now, if you broke up because you thought you could do long distance and you realize you are emotionally bereft, absolutely, see if moving closer will work. But whatever your reasons for breaking up, think about those reasons long and hard (and whether those reasons still exist) before agreeing to give things another go, because once you've gotten to the point of giving up on the relationship you now have that on the table of possible outcomes. It becomes easier next time to go there.

**Defensiveness or lack of accountability.** It is not uncommon for someone who was raised in an environment that didn't feel safe (whether that's physical or emotional safety) to not exhibit healthy habits when it comes to conflict. A lack of accountability (defensiveness, deflecting blame, or stonewalling) after having hurt others can sometimes be a symptom of narcissism. This is a definite red flag, because no partnership can withstand someone who is always right at the expense of the other.

Maybe, though, this person shuts down emotionally when confronted about the small annoyances that occur between people, because they never felt safe to be honest about uncomfortable feelings like anger or disappointment. These people might be quick to accept blame or capitulate in an effort to derail or short-circuit further discussion so as to leap-frog to a less contentious state of being. This defensiveness or disengagement may actually be a yellow flag of caution. It may indicate that this person isn't immune to your feelings but is unsure how to respond to conflict in a healthy, productive way. Be gracious and caring when discussing points of contention with these partners, and give them the space to grow and feel safe expressing their messy feelings with you.

That all said, if a person blames their exes for the failure of every past relationship, this is a giant red flag.

**Love bombing.** Conversely, if someone showers you with gifts and words of affirmation but these aren't backed by loving acts of service or kindness, or their compliments lack specificity, they may be love bombing—particularly if the gifts and over-the-top devotion happen very early in the relationship. Look at the warning signs of narcissistic control in a relationship. (There's a list in the appendix.)

I'm not saying expressions of infatuation and excitement are necessarily love bombing. But if they feel too good to be true, overly practiced, smooth, or make us feel overwhelmed, it's time to pause and ask a friend for an objective opinion.

**Controlling behavior.** Love bombing is, oddly enough, an early form of controlling behavior. Unfortunately, it is often the carrot before the stick in unhealthy relationships. It encourages us to let down our guard, but also is the foundation for later gaslighting. What do you mean, I'm not kind to you? Didn't I do all those nice things?

Controlling behavior can be insidious and can be dismissed as having jealous tendencies, but here's what I will say: It's normal to ask about what your partner's plans are for the week out of curiosity or in order to mesh schedules. It's not normal to expect or demand a partner location-share, check-in during work hours, account for every minute of their non-working/sleeping activities, or provide detailed information about where and how they spend their money. If a partner is demanding this level of surveillance, this isn't a partnership, it's a hostage situation. These behaviors don't speak to someone who wants to keep you "safe" but to someone who wants to keep you under their thumb, socially, emotionally, or financially. Worse, if they discourage you from spending time with your family or friends, this is an attempt to isolate you from your support systems and anyone who might be able to view your relationship objectively. Run, don't walk, away from this person. Controlling behavior and its sister jealousy are often the first warning signs of abusive control.

**Jealousy.** Now, hear me out. Jealousy in and of itself isn't necessarily a red flag so much as a flag of caution. Take some time to navigate this space. Jealousy wielded as means of control or shaming is definitely a red flag, but often jealousy is an indication that a partner is feeling insecure. If we are insecure because our very real observations are being dismissed? Red flag. If our partner is feeling a type of way because of past trauma, that's an opportunity to talk, to reassure, and to work through triggering scenarios to discuss what would help them feel less anxious. If anyone is triggering your jealousy/insecurity to keep you off-balance? Reddest of flags.

**You or your partner exhibit contempt, disdain, sarcasm, or indifference**. These are the four horsemen of the death of any relationship. It is said that observers can predict whether a couple will succeed long-term with substantial accuracy just by counting the proportion of positive versus negative comments about the other in a conversation. Even if spoken in jest, cutting humor erodes the bond between people. It takes four positive comments to counteract the erosive nature of a single negative comment. Words matter especially those we share with those we purport to love. Use them wisely, but also when someone shows who they are? *Believe them.*

**They treat those from a lower social position with contempt or dismissiveness.** The manner in which someone treats an individual who has no power over them tells a lot about their character. Observe how your partner treats service people, the elderly, children, and animals. There will inevitably be a day where by virtue of illness, financial situation, or emotional state that you will be the one with less power, and that attitude—whether kind or indifferent—will be your experience.

**Your partner would be perfect if only [change you'd like to see.]** Never stay in a relationship with the expectation the other party will change for you. Ask yourself, instead, if who they are *right now*, today, is someone you can accept *as is.* Does this person bring out the best in you… or not?

This applies to both big and small things, but don't expect anyone is going to radically change their religious beliefs, political views, sense of morality, cleanliness, attentiveness, or love language. I say, don't expect it. If the other person goes off and makes radical changes in their life independent of your relationship, you are free to consider them as they are at that new point in time, but you know what they say about expectations: they are simply premeditated resentments.

Change has to come from within and must be made independent of anyone else's desires or it isn't sustainable. If you are changing for someone or something else and not for yourself you are attempting to meet another's conditions for love—and that's not true love.

This isn't to say that first impressions are everything and that if someone new doesn't meet our preconceived notions of what we're looking for we should reject them. First impressions are just that: a first impression. I wouldn't have swiped right on my husband, but we've been together 38 years. Everything I based my first impression on has changed with time, evolution, and a good haircut. But the man he is at his core? Still 1000% there. To be honest, it's probably a good thing that we didn't feel immediate sparks for one another. It allowed us the space to get to know one another as people and friends. It was through that process that we realized we were compatible, and from there? Sparks.

**If you can't be your true authentic, quirky self**, that's the biggest red flag of all. It means you don't feel safe to be you or you haven't done the work to feel proud and confident in being you. Or you know that the you you are is not what that other person wants in a partner. How can we possibly judge if we are a match if we are pretending to be something we are not or not something that we are?

---

*Sidenote: If you've ever been told you exhibit any of the above red flags, or if you have a history of failed relationships and are wondering why that might be, consider that you might be the common denominator. Work on ensuring you are bringing your best, most confident, most humble, evolved and emotionally available self to your relationships. If you aren't in a place to be a good partner, how will you ever find one?*

---

## GREEN FLAGS

Not long ago my husband and I went to one of his transplant center check-ups. (More on that story later.) We've been in each other's lives for 38 years by this point and married for 33, so it's no stretch to say we've gone through some stuff.

We were chatting and chuckling over inane things when the nurse came in to take his vitals, and half-way through, she turned to us and said, "What's your secret?" We looked at each other, confused. "I'm guessing you've been together for a long time; you seem happy. I just got engaged. What's your secret?"

We looked at each other for a moment, and I shrugged, and finally said, "We make each other laugh."

Whether you aspire to monogamy or not, I think everyone who enters into a relationship hopes it goes well, feels good, and lasts. We as humans put a lot of pressure on finding "The One" or at least "The One for Now" and there's a lot of talk about sexual chemistry (important if it's important for you) and less on the question of: is this someone I genuinely enjoy spending time with?

Fundamentally, that's what any life partner is, a built-in cohort with whom to share life, so green flags will differ by what matters to the parties within each relationship. That said, and in no particular order, the key areas to consider for whether two people are compatible are generally whether you align in:

1) Core values/religious views

2) Political views (insofar as they reflect your core values)

3) Curiosity/Industriousness (do you like to explore/learn new things/travel? Do you value getting things done? Sacrificing personal time to achieve career objectives? Being chill and go with the flow?)

4) Communication styles (this can be improved or brought into alignment with therapy)

5) Love languages (which lie at the heart of how we express and experience appreciation and acceptance)

6) Sexual compatibility and the ways you enjoy experiencing intimacy

7) Sense of humor

8) Where you see yourselves living geographically and at what standard of living you find comfortable/desirable

9) Whether you see yourselves having children and/or pets (Sharing your space with any living thing outside of one another pulls attention from each other.)

10) If yes to above children/pets, do you share similar parenting ideologies, and are you open to navigating any differences?

11) Have you shared your individual dreams for travel, career, and more, and are these dreams attainable whilst in relationship with one another?

12) Should your partner experience a disability, illness, accident, setback, addiction, or trauma, would you feel it an honor or a burden to care for them, assist them, or walk that journey to recovery with them?

13) If your partner is presented with an opportunity that fulfills a dream but requires a sacrifice from you (moving, etc.) would you gladly accept that for them without resentment?

14) Finally, do you have a shared ideal trajectory for your relationship which is comfortable for both/all parties?

The old saying "opposites attract" may be true for sexual attraction and the excitement that comes with spending time with someone unlike ourselves, but those in successfully long-term relationships usually align or complement one another on most of these measures. Conflict is great for getting the blood pumping, but terrible for a good night's sleep.

Before committing formally to any long-term relationship, it's ideal to overcome adversity together or at least witness firsthand how each party behaves when *not* at their best. This is true of romantic partnerships but also platonic friendships.

---

*"A friend is someone who knows the song in your heart and can sing it back to you when you have forgotten the words."* ~ C.S. Lewis

---

Commit your time, attention, and affection to those who not only take the time and effort to learn your innermost truths but also stand beside you and support you when you falter. But also, treasure those who know you well enough to know when you can do better and can tell you these hard truths in ways you can hear them. These people are invaluable for growing into our best selves, and being in a relationship which allows for this vulnerability and honesty bodes well for its longevity—whether platonic or romantic.

The best people to judge whether someone is a good fit or worthy of us is probably our close family and friends. Listen to them.

---

*A healthy relationship is one in which we consistently and with specificity show appreciation for one another.*

---

One final enormous waving green flag for any relationship is the ability to show appreciation and gratitude for the character and actions of one another. If we verbalize our gratitude for the ways in which this other person enhances our life or makes us a better person, we are reinforcing in our own mind both the importance of this person and this relationship as well as making them feel seen and valued. So, thank your partner for noticing things about you, for doing small kindnesses or tasks, for the way in which they behave with you and others, because gratitude is a self-fulfilling prophecy.

## THE ART OF FLIRTING

***The Art of Flirting—a poem***

To flirt is an art.
It is to dance
in front of our grandmother
whilst conveying romantic interest to another
without being creepy
or too awkward
or so subtle
as to be friend-zoned.
Which is all to say
I hope I shall become a master of this art
before I am too old
to appreciate its rewards.

I'm going to say it. Flirting has become an increasingly lost art in today's overly-sexualized and hyper-gendered and toxic social culture, and it's honestly a shame, because to flirt and be flirted with is one of life's universal simple pleasures.

Yes, I absolutely understand that too many people don't understand the *art* of flirting, and that has given it a bad name. But flirting isn't about overt sexuality or objectification and all about confident connection, light-hearted *noticing,* and the mutual awareness of and intentional playing with ambiguity.

Double entendres are fine and a classic form of flirting, but they are dicey unless a true romantic connection has already been established. What I'm talking about is flirting with strangers. Flirting on first dates. Flirting with men and women and nonbinary friends and acquaintances.

One cannot enter a flirtation ham-fisted and emotionally unaware. That's cat-calling and, honestly, verbal assault. To flirt is to play with language but also to be observant of what makes another person special, unique, or humanly attractive. Whatever is said must remain socially acceptable to say in a room with one's grandmother, but the eye contact, the slight smile, the *delivery* is what transforms a banal comment into flirtation.

*"I've always enjoyed watching the stars."*

It is something two platonic friends could say to one another. It is also something that could be lent context and flirtatious overtones if whispered following a scene in a movie where the characters kiss under a brilliant night sky.

Flirtation—done right—builds connection and intimacy precisely because it is subtle. The two engaged in the flirtation are required to be actively listening, observing, and waiting for the nuanced shifts in language, intonation, and body language of the other. To flirt and be flirted with is to enjoy a light-hearted or sensual intimacy with another human, and if that human doesn't want to return the romantic undertones? They should be graciously allowed to feign innocence and the exchange should return to being a banal conversation in front of one's grandmother. No harm, no foul.

But do learn to flirt. Practice the crinkle-eyed flashing grin, the light-touch of a playful comment before dashing away into nonchalance. It is a dance as old as time and an excellent way to hone emotional intelligence and active listening skills.

Flirt without expectation but for the sheer joy of connecting with others. I promise it's worth it.

## KISS A LOT OF FROGS

I may well get pushback on this, but I'm a firm believer in broadly dating, socializing, whatever-you-want-to-call-it before committing to a long-term partner. Get out there. Drink the coffee. Do the dancing. Make the mistakes. (Use protection. Be smart about telling friends where you are. You know the drill.) Better yet, go out and get your heart broken at least once. I promise, it will hurt like hell, but that experience is going to teach you *so* much beyond how to be gentle and empathetic when it's you who needs to do the heartbreaking. It will teach you how resilient you really are, and what you don't want in a partner, because I'm going to guess that when you were with that person who left you, you never quite felt like you could be totally yourself. There was something about yourself you were hiding or keeping protected, or a truth you weren't facing.

Our future partner is going to not only dig deep to uncover all our secrets but they will do so in a way that makes us want to reveal our vulnerabilities and trust that our soft spots will be handled with the utmost of care, our dreams supported, and our traumas soothed and understood.

Dating helps us figure out who we are when in a relationship, what works for us in terms of intimacy and communication, and it helps us identify sooner whether a new someone is a potential good match. It also, let's be honest, allows us to explore what it is to be partnered with different personalities and bodies, to enjoy the variety of learning all about another person before choosing *this one.*

Dating also helps us discern whether a long-term commitment or monogamous relationship is our thing, and that's wildly useful information going forward so we don't inadvertently mislead others or ourselves.

Should you move in together? Sure, but it will be easier if the decision is based on a mutual desire and readiness to do so and is not primarily dictated for practical reasons, like someone's lease is expiring. And while an expiring lease might be just the moment to initiate the conversation about whether moving in together is the right next step, if it's within three months of meeting, it might be a bit soon. I'm not saying it won't work, but becoming roommates early in a romantic relationship can muddle the dynamic and rub the sheen of infatuation off the relationship before it's time. Are you ready to see this person clip their toenails? If not, it's too soon.

## IDENTIFYING "THE ONE"

So, you are hoping to find a long-term partner! You've done all the work to make yourself whole, happy, well-adjusted, and as trauma and addiction-free as you can get at this point in your life. How do we match you with your perfect partner?

Just kidding. So, you *exist* today and met someone you fancy and they fancy you back. Great! This is the reality. Sure, maybe you've done some therapy or have tucked away some savings, but the truth is you have a dead plant on the windowsill that you haven't gotten around to tossing, or you feel guilty about tossing it because you should be able to nurse it back to life, or you have so many plants your friends feel like they're walking into a rainforest when they visit, or you are allergic to plants, or you name all your plants as characters from your favorite anime. <deep inhale> The reality is that we are all quirky and different, and we haven't even left the topic of plants.

But maybe you and your fancy someone have moved past plants. Maybe you've learned a lot of wonderful things about each other, and you've hung out so often you are beginning to wonder if this person is "the one."

And, with luck, maybe they are wondering the same thing about you.

What I will say is that any pondering on the topic isn't something you can even hope to begin to answer until you've spent weeks or months together. Don't tell me you "knew" instantly. Perhaps you are many-years married and happy about your whirlwind courtship and elopement, and I will believe you had an amazing connection, enviable chemistry, and you got lucky. There's nothing wrong with that, but *knowing* takes time.

I had been dating my now husband for six weeks when I invited him to come to my house for Christmas (his family was out of town for the holiday.) It was only then, surrounded by my family in all its holiday chaos that I began to feel that maybe this guy was something extra special. My sister, God love her, at the end of his stay said with true sisterly snark, "If you two break up, can we keep him?" This felt like a good omen for him if not for me.

Nevertheless, it wasn't until eighteen to twenty-four months of dating that I felt that, yes, I could definitely see myself committing long-term to this man. It took him another year and a half to come to the same conclusion, but we were young.

In those early years of dating, though, we got to see beyond the initial gloss of infatuation. We had the chance to see each other when we were sick, frustrated, annoyed, or sad and were able to see how the other responded to our less-than-best selves.

It gave us the opportunity to truly sit with the idea of this being our forever person. Could we accept each other's flaws or would they be our undoing? Had we had the conversations about the future and how we envisioned it unfolding and did those visions align? Had we, in our time together, grown together as a functioning unit or were there cracks we were ignoring that threatened to push us apart?

We should never enter into a relationship expecting the other person to change for us, because they either will refuse to or agree to change and become resentful for being made to be someone or something they hadn't independently chosen to be. Yet, we all do change over time. I wouldn't say that we become someone else, but more often more ourselves. Our veneer wears off over time, and if under the shy exterior we were goofy and quirky, expect more of that to come out as we grow more comfortable. If we have a sarcastic side, be wary of that turning cynical or caustic.

I think of looking for "the one" as each of us hungry for dinner and being told that what we choose is the dinner we will eat from this point forward. Some will want tacos. Another is into burgers. Maybe we choose pizza. Ideally, we'd be served our favorite pizza with extra sauce, olives, and pepperoni. We would especially like to find just the right crust and the perfect savory sauce. A little cheddar to jazz up the mozzarella.

Even with pizza there's variability. Say we "date" lots of pizza, because that's our jam, and finally find one with the perfect crust, the most amazing sauce, a little cheddar just like we'd hoped for, and even olives and pepperoni. And onions? We didn't ask for onions. We're not against onions, but sure. Have at it!

But maybe that extra topping is anchovies. And we're allergic to them. Or this pizza has everything *but* olives.

Should we reject the pizza because it has everything but one of our favorite toppings. Is a pizza perfect if it includes a topping that we can't stand? We shouldn't expect someone who comes with anchovies to become our perfect pizza. They are, by definition, not our perfect pizza. But if they come with something extra, or lack one small thing, ask yourself if that something can be found elsewhere in your life or social sphere.

When dating, you might try a few different types of "cuisine" before you decide one is definitely your favorite. Or maybe you learn that you aren't meant to choose just one. This is all valuable information.

But if you decide you like pizza, start dating your pizzas! Figure out what your non-negotiables are. But if there's one topping difference and everything else is perfect for you, consider that may well be *your* pizza.

Finding "the one" is finding someone who makes you feel secure in expressing your true nature, feelings, and interests and having someone not want to change any of that about you. They will not be perfect in all ways, but—newsflash—neither are you. That special person is someone who loves you without condition and with whom you share that sentiment.

I cannot promise you that "the one" is forever. They may be "the one for now". But, so long as you are both honest about what you are feeling, you can move forward or apart with grace and kindness.

Ultimately, it doesn't matter what the other person brings to the table or the boxes they check on an imaginary list. The only thing that truly matters is how they make you *feel.* Full stop.

## LOVE VS. LUST

A corollary question to finding that someone special is differentiating between chemistry and something more lasting.

This isn't to say that we won't feel sparks with that special someone, but the question I see posed is often how do I know whether what I'm feeling is infatuation, chemistry, lust… or love?

And I honestly puzzled over this for a bit, because often it really isn't clear for a while. Sometimes that initial spark simply needs time to become something *more.* But then I realized that looking at the issue as a purely romantic question over complicates it a bit.

So, let's take a step back a bit and talk about relationships and emotions more generally. It has been said that there are two basic emotions: fear and love. Regardless of whether you believe that premise, I want you to for the purpose of this exercise. Now, make a list or name the feelings you feel or your sense of being when you are fearful. Don't overthink it, just ask yourself, "What is it like when I feel fear?" Do another list for when you are feeling love. I'm expecting that the first emotion is anxiety-producing, isolating, stressful, heart-racing, unpredictable, unsettling. The other, you likely associate with a sense of calm, safety, warmth, confidence, or openness. Now, think about the relationship you are in. How do you feel when you are with that person? When you are apart or leave their presence, how does that make you feel? Do you feel brighter, stronger, safer being in relationship with them? Or do you describe your times together as wild, electric, nerve-wracking, hot and cold, insecure, or exhausting?

What we often call "chemistry" is more commonly rooted in unpredictability, newness, and excitement. If chemistry is the main driver of a connection, over time it will tend to fade and may devolve into unhealthy patterns of jealousy, control, anxiety, or manipulation. Love? It becomes the opposite. The presence of love is grounding, our safe haven, a place we can be wholly and unapologetically our authentic selves. If we are hiding a part of our personality when we are with someone? It's not yet love. If we are feeling unsafe to be our authentic self because of past disapproval or reactions, it never will be until we've healed that past trauma.

We have to have the courage to say "no" to the wrong people in order to give ourselves the chance to find the *right* person.

## HOW ROMANTIC LOVE MATURES

A lot of us will have heard of the seven-year-itch, that point in a romantic relationship where the sheen of excitement has worn off and the day-to-day mundanity of real life makes people doubt whether their partnership is the best it could be. It is at this point where most people will say, "Well, marriage takes work!" And I would counter this with: commitment isn't about toughing it out so much as seeing it through. It is less about toil and more about *intention*.

Two things can be true: long-term partnerships can take effort and attention, and there are no perfect partners only people who are perfectly flawed in such a way that they are perfect for each other.

For most couples the sexual chemistry of new love and infatuation changes with time as we become more familiar with our partner, but so does the comfort of knowing what our partner enjoys and the ability to voice our own needs and desires. That said, one piece of advice that certain traditions build into the marriage preparation process that I believe would behoove everyone to consider is to engage in premarital couples counseling. It doesn't matter if you feel perfectly suited, schedule a session or two anyway. Work on setting your partnership up with the absolute best and most solid foundation and communication skills you can muster. Have a skilled outsider coach you through discussing the tricky bits you may have glossed over with the intent to "think about that later."

Absolutely, yes, thousands of couples have done just fine without this preparation, but as one of those "just fine" couples, I can see, in hindsight, how we would have benefited from some frank discussions upfront. Some digging into the gnarly bits. We managed and we stumbled through the rough parts, but given how accepted counseling is today, this feels like a sound investment in every partnership whether you are just starting out or have been at it a while.

Marriage overall is a bit like navigating the mythical fire swamp. There are known pitfalls: finances, kids, boredom. All of these can be navigated with *honest and respectful communication*. The key to making it through the rough times is to acknowledge that you are usually *both* going through things and to be open about them, clearly communicate what you'd like to see addressed and how, and to be loving and generous with your grace and understanding.

Conflict in general often pits us against each other. In a partnership, it's better to align with our partner in such a way that we are facing our issues as a team, not as opposing combatants. By treating issues as something to be faced together, we are signaling to our partner that we value their input which makes us both more content and, side benefit, interested in physical intimacy.

Here's where popular culture and depictions of couples over time can make us doubt whether we are "normal". We might have bought into the myths that couples naturally are less interested in sex over time (not true), that spontaneous sex is the best sex (also not true), and that issues around physical intimacy are purely physiological (sometimes but not always true.)

Physical intimacy within a long-term partnership is less about spontaneous moments of passionate desire and more about being responsive to opportunities to express affection and physicality. No, sex with our partner will likely not look the same as it did before the kids, the house, and the nine-to-five job, but as long as we continue to respond to our partner's bids for attention, validation, and common interest the desire for intimacy should remain. Emotional intimacy is the key to physical intimacy. It's also the only way to be vulnerable enough to address medical or emotional barriers should they come up.

## THE BUSINESS OF MARRIAGE

We talk a lot about marriage, getting married, who to marry, but we talk very little about the fact that marriage, outside of any religious or emotional sacrament or vow, is a *financial* commitment and legal contract. To get married is to take on another's emotional burdens and life dreams but also their real-world debts. To be married early in life is to commit to another who might make it nearly impossible to extricate ourselves from that relationship, because of the financial hardship of doing so. Likewise, mixing finances as two partners outside of marriage can teach us a lot about how this person will behave within the confines of a financial partnership.

Divorce is expensive and difficult as much because of emotionally separating from another person but because of the complexity of deciding how to separate the financial lives of two individuals and their commitments and contributions.

It's all well and good to think about marriage as a joyful union between two people who love one another, and I'm all for that. It has given my life great meaning and support, but you can experience a joyful union without marriage, so if you are not fully and soberly considering the financial aspects of what it means to marry another, hit the pause button. I'll wait.

## DIVORCE: CALLING IT A DAY ON A RELATIONSHIP

We've all heard the "conscious uncoupling" phrase by now, and as much as it induced eye-rolling, it isn't a terrible idea if the circumstances allow. A lot of people, though, are blindsided by divorce or a breakup, so how do you see it coming? How should we communicate a desire to part ways? What are the ethics and nuances and logistics?

Let's get this out of the way: no one enters into a long-term commitment expecting it to end. We enter partnerships, usually, with enthusiasm, optimism, and a can-do attitude. But unresolved issues, outside pressures and stressors, addictions of all varieties, and simply growing apart *do* happen and will often erode the foundation of a relationship.

---

*Indifference is the death knell to any relationship.*

---

So, what are some hints your relationship is in trouble? Indifference. Whether expressed or felt as disdain, annoyance, or contempt, indifference is the death knell of any relationship. You might feel it in realizing that you are no longer interested in your partner or their happiness or wellbeing, you might feel hostility or resentment toward activities they engage in or people they spend time with. Or, you may be feeling or hearing your partner express such feelings about you. In either case: these are alarm bells ringing. If you choose to ignore them, your relationship will eventually end.

If you choose to address the issue(s), you may be able to save the relationship or at least part cordially, but the best time to seek outside counseling or assistance is when these issues start to cause friction but have not yet bled into indifference or outright hostility.

If your communication styles are what is in conflict, this may also cause a rocky road in parting ways, but that was also covered in red flags.

If you've decided to part ways whether married or not and you feel safe to do so, please tell this person face to face or at least via a phone call. Never, ever, break up over text or DM or any other means where the other party does not have the ability to respond or ask questions in real time. It will never end there, and you are subjecting the other to the cruel space of *not knowing*. Yes, it's grueling to break up in person and to listen to the other party's hurt feelings, but *as long as it is safe to do so*, it is the compassionate thing to do and will give the other person closure.

Make arrangements then and there for how you might handle any logistics relating to the breakup in terms of finances, leases, furnishings, pets, or set a time to discuss such logistics when the other party has had time to process their emotions.

Moving through such times is emotionally grueling for everyone, and you may feel hurt or guilt or shame that you didn't make it work or did something the other party cannot forgive, but as adults we owe anyone we've been intimate with the consideration of our honesty and compassion.

What we do not owe them is a relationship going forward unless there are kids or pets involved and then we must find it within ourselves to be civil for the sake of the children/pets.

If pets are involved, I don't care who brought them into the relationship or wanted them. The pets should remain with whomever they are most bonded provided it is safe and practical to do so and they will be well-cared for. Any bonded pets should not be separated unless they were brought into the relationship from the separate parties and have spent more time apart than together. Yes, it is hard for you, but your pets had no say in how your relationship went and the impact on them should be minimized.

Children should have a say in where they live and with whom once they are able to vocalize their preference and should not be unduly influenced by either parent (provided it is safe for them to choose either household.) They are neither pawns nor counselors and should never be treated as such.

The greatest kindness a parent can show a child is how to move through this life with grace and compassion, and how to be present for one's self while also being aware of the impact of one's actions on others. No matter how young they are, children always remember. Act accordingly.

PART 3

# COMMUNICATION

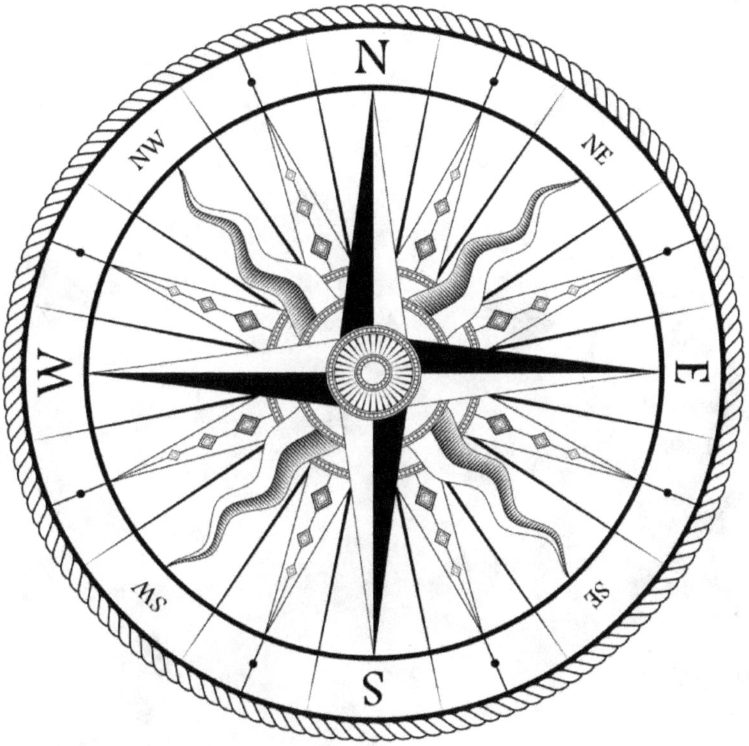

# Chapter 6

## COMMUNICATION IS KEY

### UNDERSTANDING COMMUNICATION STYLES

Growing up the youngest of four, I was no stranger to spats between siblings. Personality clashes, ideological differences, and who left the kitchen a mess, were all hashed out the same way: we got irritated, tracked down the source of our irritation, voiced (usually loudly) our irritation, they rebutted, and we stomped off. Ten minutes later we'd grudgingly ask if they wanted tea as we were heating water.

This method of openly and immediately addressing issues as they presented themselves led me to the mistaken assumption that that's how conflict was handled by everyone. You vented, they either apologized or told you why you were wrong, everyone got it off their chest, and you moved on with your lives.

Then I met my now husband. Granted it was some time before we had our first disagreement, but I remember how it went. I vented. He clammed up, shut down, and walked away.

As you can imagine, this was less than satisfying.

I bustled after him and restated my annoyance. He gave me the silent treatment.

What I failed to understand is that he was brought up in a household that was extremely conflict-avoidant. To actively confront another was unheard of and caused him to emotionally shut down. I had to learn a new way of communicating my feelings when I was annoyed or disagreed in such a way that he could hear me if I wanted any resolution.

During less fraught moments, I finally asked about his behavior, spoke about where I was coming from, and we both gained insight into how the other perceived and handled conflict.

There's a lot more to the story in terms of family dynamics going on here, but what I will say is that when there is conflict in a relationship, it's vital to have the presence of mind to recognize when you are no longer in communication but are in conflict. That's the time to pause and call a time-out, because unless we are seeking resolution, we are harming our relationship.

## FIGHTING FAIR

No relationship conflict should involve physically touching another. If you have resorted to slapping, hitting, poking, or any other form of physically expressing your heightened emotions, that's a problem you need to step away from and ask for outside help in resolving, because it is not a safe space for either party.

(If you are on the receiving end of such abuse, please see the appendix for resources.)

Moreover, no argument should ever involve name-calling, pejorative language, swearing, or hyperbolic or blanket statements such as "*you always*" or "*you never.*" Period. These are verbal attacks and will always place the other in a defensive mode. When we use these tactics, it is too easy to slide into a moment of saying something we may well regret. Yes, even if what our partner has done betrays everything we hold dear, we should seek to take a moment to exhale. Once. Twice. Ten times. Clear our head of the insults so that we can get to expressing the core of what is making us angry.

I say this with love knowing that when we are so angry we want to hurl insults, it's usually because the other person has deeply wounded us. But if they have, and if they have no remorse or understanding of the impact of their behavior, our words won't affect them, but those same words may affect *us*. Those words may be used against us later when we want custody of our shared children or pets. They may be hurled back at us when we are even more vulnerable—twisted, gaslighting us. They may simply make us feel dirty or dragged down to a baser level we never intended to inhabit.

If we want to disagree in a way that preserves the relationship, we must discuss things with an eye toward seeking resolution, not vindication or victory.

---

*Disagreements should seek resolution, not vindication or victory.*

---

Address one issue at a time. If either party calls back to a prior and unrelated grievance? Call it out. Piling on doesn't resolve the issue, it is designed to prove that the other has a pattern of being in the wrong. And guess what? That's arguing to win, not to resolve.

## LISTENING

Years ago, my husband saw an ad in the paper for a moving sale that mentioned woodworking tools. He was looking for a bigger table saw, so he told me he planned to stop after work and he'd be home a little late.

Several hours later than I'd anticipated him, he rolled into the driveway with a small boat trailer behind the car.

Mind you, we did not own a boat.

I looked at him, looked at the boat trailer, then looked at him again.

"You probably have questions," he said.

"Many," I replied.

It turned out that the table saw he'd been considering had already sold by the time he'd arrived.

"So… you bought a boat trailer?" I asked.

"He seemed lonely," said my husband.

And then my husband told me how the man selling the trailer had recently lost his wife. None of their kids lived nearby, so it had been decided the man would move in with his son. This elderly man had been liquidating the accumulations of a lifetime, alone, in order to sell the house.

"He kept showing me around, pointing out things I might be able to use, talking about his wife. They used to go to the lake when the kids were younger. The boat was in rough shape, but I felt so bad for him, and he looked so sad… I bought the trailer."

The medical bills had been steep, and my husband wanted to help, but a lot of what was left to sell had seen better days. To preserve the man's dignity, my husband had exchanged the cash he'd brought for the table saw for a random, rusty boat trailer.

He had listened enough to have heard that the memories of those days on the lake with family were what that elderly man saw when he looked at that trailer, so my husband valued it accordingly.

We never did use that boat trailer, and that's okay. That wasn't what that evening wandering that man's small property had been about. It had been about valuing human connection.

And listening.

One of the most valuable skills to cultivate is to be a good listener. I say this as someone who routinely interrupts people, thinks about what I am going to say next, forgets people's names the millisecond after hearing them and more. Basically, this is one area I know is a weakness and one I am working hard to improve upon.

I think we all know what good listening looks like. We know it when *we* are heard, seen, validated. We know it based on the eye contact, the pointed and topical questions we're asked, and the way there is often a short pause after we finish speaking. A good listener knows that to listen is to make space for another to find the words, to name their feelings, and to begin to solve their own dilemma in the environment of acceptance and safety created when we truly and meaningfully listen.

A good listener listens with curiosity, not to inform or correct. They seek to respond, not to react or rebut, and that takes a moment or two of processing. On the receiving end we know the difference.

If I am feeling emotionally unsettled or dysregulated and unable to listen without feeling reactive, I try to zoom out enough from the situation to a place of emotional neutrality. I try to see not just through my own lens but through my partner's or the other person's lens and then, further still, try to reach a point where I can see the dynamic of the two (or more) of us at once. From this space, I feel I am truly able to listen. This is the place in which I can listen and respond with loving neutrality, because I am seeing the situation and conversation from a larger context. (More on this topic later.)

None of this is to say that someone who enthusiastically chatters back or shares a similar story of their own isn't listening. Your words may have sparked excitement in them they wish to share. Or, perhaps, it feels like something they, too, have encountered, and they hope to share their, similar, story to validate that you are not alone in your feelings or experience.

Communication can feel messy and confusing, but if we train ourselves to observe body language cues, to self-regulate our responses enough to see if they are adding to or hijacking a conversation, and if we listen with the intent of being wholly present with someone, communication will be our ticket to connection.

## THE POWER OF APOLOGY

Many (many) years ago when I was about five years old, I came to be in possession of a suction cup dart. As a young person without a packed schedule, I proceeded to test the relative suction-ability of my home.

I eventually found myself outside, suction cup dart in hand testing the bricks around the outdoor fireplace, the wooden railing by the side steps, and then hit gold once I reached the aluminum siding.

My little arm swung in for contact. *Schtuck.*

I yanked the dart off the wall again. *Thwact.*

Satisfied with these sounds, I walked along swinging in for a landing, *schtuck*, and yanking it away again, *thwact.*

This mindless repetition carried me around the side of the house to the side door. *Schtuck. Thwact. Shtuck. Thwact.*

But then I reached the side door, and as my little arm, propelled by a total lack of awareness, swung my fisted dart toward the storm door glass, I instead heard *crash.*

I don't know for sure, but I'm not convinced they made the glass of storm door panes out of tempered material in those days. All I know is that in the moments after the glass shattered on contact, my mother's face came rushing from the other side of the kitchen. Her "what happened?" was drowned out by my tearful "I'm sorry" but the dart in my fist probably told her everything she needed to know.

She brusquely ordered me to my room so she could clean up, and I stepped through the glass and ran up to my bed, chastised, regretful, and… bloody?

Was that blood on my hand?

I remember staring at the small scratch on my hand, squeezing it to assure myself I wasn't imagining I'd been hurt, and then crying anew that my dear mother was more fussed with cleaning the mess I'd made then attending to her own, injured child.

I was slightly dramatic like that.

In reality, it was probably less than twenty minutes before my mother came to my room and sat on the bunk next to me. Her manner was calmer now, her voice gentler when she asked if I was okay.

"I didn't mean to do it," I said.

She nodded. "I know. It was an accident. I'm sorry I yelled. I was worried you had been hurt and upset about the mess."

I held up my injured hand and pointed sadly at the scratch. She asked if I needed a Band-Aid for it. I nodded, and just like that, not only was my hand okay, but so was the bond with my mother.

Years later, as a mother myself, I wasn't nearly as generally calm as I remember my sainted mother being. I was often overwhelmed, frazzled, overtired, and hangry. I was not my best self, and I knew it.

There were times I adored my kids but was equally overwhelmed by them, and I became "yelly mom." I don't share this with pride, but with honesty.

I distinctly remember one instance where my son was simply being his beautiful, exuberant self, and I snapped. I watched his face crumble, his shoulders deflate, and, in that moment, I felt like the worst mother to ever walk the earth.

I put myself in a time-out, sat with my feelings, and knew what I had to do.

I found my son quietly playing, chastised into silence, and asked if I could sit with him. He nodded.

I blew out a breath, looked him in the eye, and said, "I'm so sorry I lost my cool before. You did nothing wrong and definitely didn't deserve to have me yelling at you. I was frustrated and overwhelmed by other things, and I took it out on you, and that wasn't fair. I am so sorry."

His eyes welled with tears, and that young boy gave me the greatest gift that day. He gave me a hug.

We told each other we loved each other, and as I sat with him and asked to join his play time, humbled but grateful to be given another chance to be the mom I wanted to be, I realized that I was learning right alongside my son. A heartfelt apology has the power to heal.

There are those who believe that adults, especially parents, should never apologize to children. Or, some who hijack their own apology to chastise the child for "making them mad." What I say to that is: if you value a relationship, any relationship, you will act accordingly. Wounds inflicted without apology seldom heal.

We are all fallible beings and not always our best selves. We will inevitably hurt others over the course of time. A genuine, heartfelt, humble apology works wonders to heal those wounds in several ways.

**For the one *receiving* the apology:**

1) An apology which specifically names and recognizes the way(s) we've been wounded makes us feel seen and heard.
2) An apology validates our feelings, our reality, and our perspective.
3) An apology, freely given, assures us that we and the relationship are valued and worth the effort of making amends.

**For the one *giving* the apology:**

1) An apology given with a humble heart removes our ego from the original conflict which allows us to recognize how our actions—good and bad—affect others.
2) An apology unburdens us of the weight of trying to pretend that the harm was "no big deal" or somehow "deserved" by the wounded party. (Gaslighting ourselves.) We can own our flaws and actions, vow to do better, and forgive ourselves for being human.
3) An apology moves us to a space of both vulnerability and courage. It is not weakness to apologize but bravery to face our own flaws, admit to them, seek to make amends for how we've harmed, and allow those we've hurt to express themselves honestly.

4) An apology is a sign of emotional maturity and love. Rather than defensiveness or deflection, humility releases us. We have given the power back to the one harmed so that the relationship can be rebalanced.

## HOW (NOT) TO APOLOGIZE

The point of apologizing for our hurtful words or actions is to preserve and heal our connections with others. There's a right way and a wrong way to apologize as most of us know from experience.

In no particular order:

- Apologies should be specific and name the ways in which we know we have hurt someone. If we aren't sure what we're apologizing for, it's time to step back and assess the interaction, the dynamics of the relationship, and the other person.

- Apologies should never include a "but." A genuine apology doesn't hedge its bets or get in subtle digs. This is the time to atone for the *specific thing(s)* we did that hurt the other person. They can apologize for their poor behavior separately.

- Likewise, if you are a parent or adult and a child comes to apologize, it is not a teachable moment to point out how they might have behaved or acted differently. That child is seeking to repair the relationship. Allow that to happen with grace. The lessons can wait for another conversation.

- A sincere apology never gaslights. This is our one opportunity to acknowledge that what we said or did hurt another. Their feelings are valid. Their perception and perspective are valid.

Any words to dismiss their feelings, to call out their reaction as being "too sensitive", or otherwise gaslight them about the impact of our actions is going to do more harm than no apology at all.

- An apology is never a time to explain our perspective or feelings unless specifically prompted. This is about the one we harmed, not us.

- A good apology is delivered calmly, never grudgingly. It is delivered on *their* terms and in *their* timeframe. It places ego firmly on the shelf for the duration of the apology and is delivered humbly and with vulnerability. A heartfelt apology sets down the swords and shields of conflict; it meets the wounded with vulnerability and a sincere desire for reconciliation.

- Apologies should never be coerced. A child who feels safe to apologize should never be chastised. They are learning emotional maturity from us. Let's be good models.

- An apology allows space for the other person to feel their valid feelings, express their valid feelings, and to respond however they feel moved. Think of an apology as a game of tennis. You've volleyed the ball over the net. It's on their side. They now can decide to grab the ball and walk away, return it in kind, or hold onto it, bouncing it, talking about the game until they're ready to proceed. My point is: it is up to them.

- A sincere apology seeks to make amends as appropriate, to make the injured party whole again, financially and emotionally.

## RESPONDING TO AN APOLOGY

Many of us have been conditioned, when apologized to, to respond, “That’s okay.” And maybe it is, and our wound didn’t go that deep, but what if it’s not okay? What if we still feel the sting of that initial hurt despite the fact that the person who wounded us has come to us to apologize?

It's okay to respond however we are moved. It’s okay to say, “Thank you for the apology,” or, “Thank you for the apology. I appreciate it.”

These responses recognize that the apology was made, we are grateful for the effort, but there may be more that needs to be done to repair the relationship from where we are standing. It’s okay to say, “Thank you for the apology. I appreciate it. I’m going to need to think about how I want to move forward.”

Remember, when an apology is made, the ball now is in our court. We can think about how we might have played a role in the original conflict and be moved to share our own apology. Or, upon reflection, we might recognize that the person apologizing has a pattern of hurting us and, perhaps, this is when we decide we don’t want to move forward with the relationship.

## GRACE AND FORGIVENESS

As we talk about apologies, it’s an obvious segue into the topic of forgiveness. Most of us, when we are moved to sincerely apologize hope for forgiveness, right? But I want to take a moment to unpack what that means.

In my mind, forgiveness is a gift from the harmed or wounded. It is an absolution. It says, “I wipe the slate clean.” Forgiveness “forgets”.

But there are times, circumstances, where forgetting much less forgiving feels impossible. There are people who have wounded us so deeply or with such lack of care or concern, or who simply haven't even offered an apology, that it feels like it would be an additional burden to then gift this person forgiveness.

I've heard that forgiveness is a gift we give ourselves, but I am going to suggest this, instead:

---

*Forgiveness wipes the slate clean.*
*It is a gift we give to those we want to remain connected to.*
*Grace accepts with loving neutrality.*
*It is a gift we give ourselves when that connection has been severed and we want the freedom to move on.*

---

Let me explain.

If forgiveness wipes the slate clean, grace recognizes that the slate is very much *not clean.* Perhaps the slate is broken beyond repair. Grace sees the hurts, sees the actions, acknowledges the apology (if any) and accepts them all as having happened. That is all. Grace accepts these things as true and valid and allows the connection, now severed, to remain so.

Grace is a gift of acceptance which frees us from being tied to history, hurtful people, and old wounds.

Grace looks at the scars of a connection and frees us from having to put in more effort. It frees the other person, too, to go forth in their own life to, hopefully, learn from the relationship and make better choices.

So, no, I don't believe we are obliged to forgive others for the ways they have harmed us. But grace? Grace is a gift of loving neutrality. It doesn't forget; it learns, frees, and moves forward.

But there are times, [illegible] giving [illegible] impossible. [illegible] openly, or with such lack [illegible] without an apology [illegible] additional [illegible] then [illegible] the person [illegible] forgiveness [illegible] going to [illegible].

---

[illegible]

---

Let me explain.

If forgiveness wipes the slate clean, [illegible] slate is very much *not* clean. Perhaps [illegible] repair. Grace sees the [illegible] apology (if any) and [illegible] If Grace accepts [illegible] connection, now severed, to [illegible].

Grace is [illegible] history [illegible].

Grace looks [illegible] having to put in more [illegible] forth in their own [illegible] make better choices.

[illegible] necessarily, but doesn't [illegible]

PART 4

# PARENTING

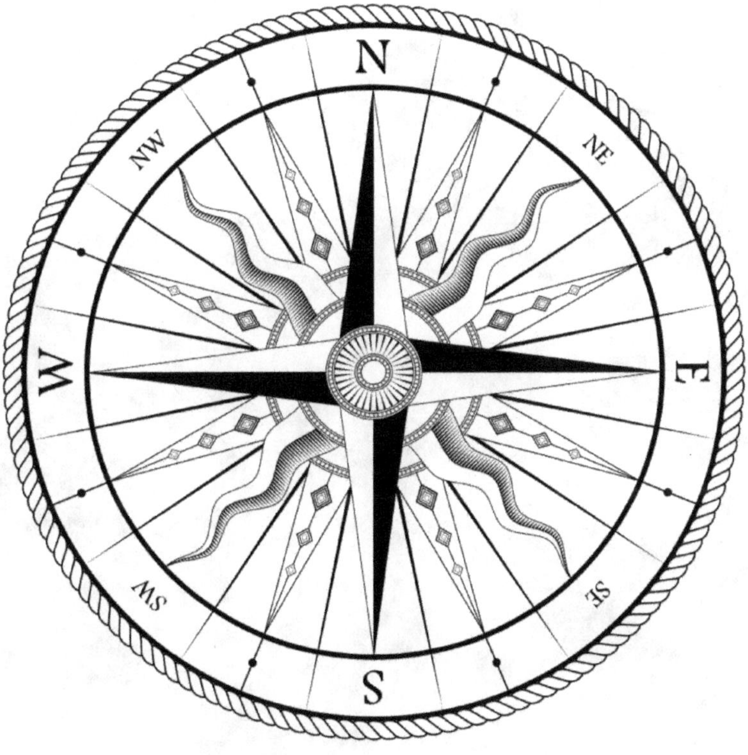

# Chapter 7

## PARENTING

You might be tempted to skip this chapter if you don't have kids or don't intend to, but I ask you to reconsider that. Much of what follows pertains as validly to adopting and raising a pet as a human. It may help you heal from or understand your own upbringing. We could all benefit from thinking about ways to better nurture and guide the youth in our lives and supporting the parents of those youth. The old saying "it takes a village" holds true. Even if we aren't around for the four a.m. feedings, we are part of the village and anyone's less sleep-deprived input is valuable to the next generation of humanity.

### WHAT DOES IT MEAN TO BE A PARENT?

I think about this sometimes when I hear someone whose relationship (or lack thereof) with a biological father has them referencing that person as a "sperm donor." Or maybe an extra close bond earns someone the honorific of "bonus mom." But what is it to be a parent if not to be the biological cause of someone else's existence? Are we dismissing "pet parents"? Foster parents? Adoptive parents? Of course not.

Yes, the technical definition of parent is biological, but there's a difference between the noun and title of *parent* and the verb and action *to parent.* Most of us understand that the *act* of parenting is to nurture, guide, or care for another. It makes perfect sense, then, that those who fill this role are parenting whether they are biologically connected or not.

Back when my son was born, I remember feeling an immense sense of responsibility toward this little human placed in my care. An older woman in my church at the time said something which resonated with me:

---

*Children are a blessing.*
*Not ours to keep,*
*but ours to care for.*

---

We as parents are caretakers. We have been gifted the opportunity to guide another human safely and securely to adulthood. It's a massive responsibility, sometimes unwittingly foisted upon us, but this *is* the role of a parent. A child isn't a possession to force into a mold of our choosing, nor are they a means of acting out our dreams for ourselves or to parade as some sort of trophy, nor should they ever be a target for our anger at the world or our circumstances. Their appearance in our lives is not something they could direct, and so they are entirely at our mercy.

Every child is a gift placed in our care. Some of us fail miserably at the task, but if we aim—no matter how we ourselves were parented—to do right by any child who appears in our life, whether human or furry or what-have-you, we are stepping up to the role of nurturer, guide, and teacher. We know that our success means this child will grow knowing they are loved and that we are willing to give them the independence they are capable of attaining with a soft place to land should they ever need it.

No child owes a parent monetarily or emotionally for their existence any more than any of us has agreed to a debt to the universe for coming into being. Our children do not owe others in their lives a relationship or displays of affection if that is not coming organically from their own desires. To demand it of them is a call to look within ourselves at what that is telling us about our own experiences, biases, or boundaries.

## BECOMING A PARENT

The road to parenthood is as varied as the children born into this world, and there is no right way or time to become a parent. My husband and I chose to be partners first and then parents later on, which came with the benefit of maturing as individuals and partners, but came at the cost of my children not knowing their grandfathers. I'm not going to sit here and tell you you are doing it wrong or not entering into the responsibility with enough gravitas if you or circumstance choose a different timeline.

What I do know is that I'm glad I waited until we both agreed it was time. Tricking or pressuring someone into becoming a parent (I'm looking at you, overzealous would-be-grandparents), no matter the circumstances, is a recipe for resentment toward both the partner and the child. No amount of sleepless nights, financial stress, or worry about colic brought any couple closer together, so never delude yourself into believing a baby will "fix" what troubles your partnership. A baby will most definitely uncover issues you didn't know you had, so before becoming a parent, should you have the choice, ask yourself and your partner (should you have one), some key questions:

1) Why am I hoping to become a parent?

2) Why is this a good time for me, personally, and us as partners, to have a child?

3) Am I/are we financially stable and able to foresee having the resources to support this child to adulthood?

4) Am I in good physical health? If not, are there steps I can take now to improve my health so I can be present and at my best to care for this child into their adulthood?

5) Am I in good mental health? Am I emotionally healthy enough to nurture another human right now? If not, how might I address my mental health status to be at my best and most present to care for this child into their adulthood?

6) Do I have the physical space or circumstances to welcome a child?

7) Do I have family, friends, or community that I know I can count on to help me with this child should I become sick, injured, disabled, or worse?

8) Have my partner and I discussed our values, parenting styles and philosophies, discipline, and any religious beliefs, and are we on the same page? Have we resolved any conflicts in these areas to our mutual satisfaction?

9) Have I ever uttered the phrase: "My parents [fill in the blank] and I turned out okay"? (Pro tip: You are probably not as okay as you may think. You probably have some things to unpack, because you are likely carrying around

some woundedness and resentment around that thing you insist you survived.)

10) Is there anything I want to do—travel, extreme sports, become an entrepreneur—that I'd be more comfortable doing before the responsibility and logistics of having a child?

11) Have I spent time around babies/children so I know I'm not idealizing the prospect of parenthood?

12) Do I have any expectations around the gender, abilities, appearance, etc. of this potential child? I'm going to gently but firmly nudge you toward therapy if you answered "yes" to this one. For your potential child, I beg of you to unpack this.

13) Finally: Do I have love for myself and love to spare?

Feel free to use this same list of questions when deciding to bring any living creature into your home with some obvious substitutions.

The reality is, few of us are in a perfect place when we become parents. And for many of us "good enough" is sometimes all we have to give. But if we are choosing whether to become parents, if we are deciding on a commitment that is going to last for the rest of our mutual lives, it seems to me that's a time to pause, take a moment for some honest heart-to-hearts and internal work before saying, "Yes, let's do this." We must be sure, to the best of our ability, it's an enthusiastic, everyone on board, "Hell, yes!" if we possibly can.

## DO THE WORK BEFORE (IF YOU CAN)

If you aren't an experiential learner, this next bit is for you.

I love my husband deeply, and we've made it through a lot of ups and downs but the one thing I wish we would have done before becoming parents is become much more intentional with our communication. There was a lot of unaddressed familial dysfunction around communication, how to handle conflict, and unspoken expectations that carried over into our partnership despite our deep love and commitment to one another. We waited eight years after we married to start having kids, but if I had it to do over again, I would poke at the bits of us that we tended to gloss over. Because having children doesn't make any issue or communication disconnect go away. Children bring chaos and stress into the world along with adorable little faces. Their presence will only magnify any issues you might have previously been able to scootch under the rug.

Work on open and honest communication now. I promise it will benefit all of you.

More broadly, we are our child's first teacher. We should be sure we've learned important life lessons and grown as appropriate before bringing a child into our world. Be the parent you wish you'd had or the one whose memory you want to live up to.

## PARENTHOOD WILL FOREVER CHANGE YOU

Becoming a parent is a transformative experience. Once you become wholly responsible for another human's welfare and well-being, there's a gravitas to your existence you'll never be without. There is a sense of having crossed over a one-way bridge. Kids don't bring happiness so much as purpose to one's life—meaning. Lessons which help us grow. I say this, because there is a persistent myth that children are a joyful blessing—and they are—but not in the every-day-is-sunshine way many portray them. Children are work! They are messy. Loud. Obstinate. Confusing. Beautiful. Delightful. Curious. Silly. Smart.

Our kids break our hearts and mend them a thousand times over their lifetime. There will be days we know we love them but wonder whether we like them. But even then, on those very hardest of days, if someone threatened our kid? We'd defend them with a Mama Bear's intensity.

Once they've grown and reached the legal age of maturity—we are still a parent. They may be sixty and we might be eighty, our caretaking roles reversed, and we will still feel like a parent and child to one another.

To become a parent is to choose to live a life whose purpose has expanded beyond the limits of one's self. Be ready to expand into this being before committing to parenthood. Once the caterpillar has taken flight as the butterfly, there's no going back.

## BIRTH AND BABIES

All birth is childbirth if a child is produced. There is no right or wrong way to bring a child into this world. Vaginal birth is childbirth. Unmedicated birth is childbirth. Medicated birth is childbirth. A cesarean-section birth is childbirth. Stillbirth is childbirth.

You have the right as a birthing person to decide what is done to you regardless of "policy." Be sure to have an advocate who knows your preferences but also be open to hearing the advice of those who are seeking the best outcome for you and your baby.

No one should be in the room the birthing person doesn't want there. Period. No discussion. Away with you, toxic people and dysfunctional family dynamics. The birthing space is sacred! This directive includes the source of sperm, any specific nursing staff, or even anyone who may have previously had permission but whom the person having the baby has decided is no longer welcome. Birth is a personal and overwhelming experience in the best of circumstances and no one has a *right* to be present except for the person giving birth and the child being born.

As natural as birth is, it is hard on a body. After birth, it takes weeks for the body to recover. Consider birth the equivalent of an ultra-marathon or major surgery (or both) and treat that body with care and respect in the days following birth. Hydrate. Rest. Ignore outside expectations. Brush your teeth. I promise it will help you feel better. Give yourself space to grow into your new role. Know that the former you still exists deep inside. Honor the body that did such amazing work.

If you are not the birthing person? Treat them with gentle care, kindness, and keep an eye on their mental health. Hormones are tricky beasts and not to be underestimated. Do not dismiss warning signs of PPD, and if you don't know what that is, now is the time to look it up and become informed.

Well-meaning and overbearing relatives alike will want to see the newborn and give advice. The non-birthing partner should be firm but gentle with boundaries and defend the sacred post-partem space. Confirm what help is welcomed and by whom. Expect to take up the "slack" of household chores the recovering partner is not currently up to doing. There is no man's work or woman's work, only housework.

As natural as breastfeeding is, it may not come naturally. It is a skill that also must be learned. If you intend to breastfeed consult a lactation consultant ASAP. I promise you that the labor and delivery nurses are good, but they may not have skills in helping to identify latch or other issues. Don't ask me how I know.

If you are unwilling or unable to breastfeed, know that the only important thing is that your baby be fed to meet their nutritional needs as is appropriate for the caregivers and the circumstances available. A breastfed baby is fed. A formula-fed baby is fed. You get the idea.

Babies should be put to sleep in such a space and in such a way that works for the baby, the parents, and is deemed safe.

Babies on a schedule can be healthy babies. Babies not on a schedule can be healthy babies.

Babies cannot be spoiled. I will repeat this:

---

*Babies cannot be spoiled.*

---

If your baby cries and you respond to it, you are communicating to that infant that they are not alone in this world, that the world will come to their aid when they are in distress, and you are building an emotional bond of trust with that infant. Feeding a hungry baby despite what time the clock says it is, soothing an overtired infant until it settles its nervous system enough to fall asleep, or changing its soiled diaper are all opportunities for you, as the caregiver, to learn to communicate with that child. There is literally no downside to responding to your baby. None. In fact, responsive caregivers foster secure attachment in babies which translates to more confident and well-adjusted adults.

My youngest was an infant when my first child was a preschooler. Naturally, I couldn't nap when the baby napped, because I was running around doing things, like keeping my toddler from falling down stairs or drinking poison. So, baby number two spent the first years of her life in a baby sling. Nap time? She snoozed while I grocery-shopped, did chores around the house, and played with her brother.

When she grew to be a toddler, she wasn't able to fall asleep unless draped across a human. Grandma spent many a peaceful afternoon on our couch holding our "barnacle baby," reading novels, and sipping tea.

There were plenty that warned that such a child would never learn to stand on her own much less sleep on her own, that her brother speaking for her when she was shy and hiding behind him meant she'd never speak for herself, and that by indulging her we were only setting her up for a lifetime of dependence and insecurity.

Fast forward and this same child flew to France, alone, at the age of sixteen to visit her French exchange student match and family. She took a semester abroad in college, joined her student senate at university, and has shown no signs at all of being either painfully shy or dangerously, unhealthily dependent.

This is to say, allow your babies to be babies and love them. Let the bouncing ones fall asleep in their johnny-jump-ups, allow the binkies for those that need them until they don't, and only fight the battles that make sense to fight for you and your family. If you don't *need* a strict bedtime and it only stresses everyone, then don't have one. If you need to have space to sleep and the kids aren't ready to be on their own, put a king-size mattress on the floor for a year. Do what works for your family and your babies, because we're all just trying to get by, hold down jobs, and remain relatively sane and healthy. No one is grading you on this. The only goal is to have healthy happy children grow to adulthood and to survive the process.

## NEEDING A BREAK FROM YOUR CHILD

Images of idealized parenthood are plastered all over social media and influencer accounts. Clean homes. Smiling, serene children. Matching outfits. Heartwarming scenes of baking bread or cookies together. Reality is that most of us are stressed from work responsibilities, worried about finances, overwhelmed with caregiving for pets, parents, aging homes, and any other children we might have, or waylaid with another round of norovirus running rampant through the household.

So, what if we need a break from the baby or child? What if we love them, but *in this moment* don't particularly like them? First, I'm so proud of you for admitting that you aren't your best in this moment. If you can, ask someone else to step in—a partner, relative, or friend. If there is no one else and you need a break or you'll snap or lash out? Tell your child you need a moment to calm yourself and *take it*. By stating a need for calm, taking a moment to visibly breathe, or engaging in some other self-soothing behavior you are modeling emotional regulation and teaching your child how to handle overwhelming feelings. Chances are very good it is their own inability to fully regulate their emotions or behavior that got you to this point. Only when you are calm and able to speak in a normal tone of voice should you reengage with your child.

If it's a baby you are overwhelmed by, set them in a safe location and *step away*. A baby will be absolutely fine if you step away somewhere quiet, soothe yourself, and then return in a more regulated state. If you are feeling that your baby is unsafe with you, please call a trusted friend or mental health hotline to get help for both of you. That saying "it takes a village" isn't just about caring for children. It's about the community it takes to support parents, too. You are not a bad parent for having messy feelings. Please take care of you so that you can parent your child at your best.

## POTTY TRAINING

There are entire books written on this subject, so the only thing I will say is this: toddlers and teens will rebel if you give them something to rebel against. Toddlers will potty train themselves given encouragement, proper accommodations, and time. They also smell the desperation of parents who *need* them trained for preschool or convenience. Both of my kids trained at three years of age almost to the day with less than a handful of accidents after. When they are ready, they will do it. To attempt to rush the process is to either train yourself to predict their needs or invite a battle that will leave everyone in tears. I get it, diapers are a drag and expensive, but when it comes to potty training, the one ultimately in control is the child, and don't you want them working with you and not against you?

This same approach applies to teens. It is a myth that "all teens are rebellious." Yes, they go through a developmental phase of separating from their parents and forging their own identity, and there are real and valid situations of oppositional defiance and such which are exceptions. But extreme rebelliousness? It is often a reaction to parents attempting to exert more control over their teens when they should be preparing those teens for taking control over themselves.

Ultimately, like the potty-training toddler, the teen is the one in control of their choices. Wouldn't you rather be seen as a coach, experienced elder, or guardrail instead of an obstacle?

## WE ARE ALL TODDLERS

When my first-born was a toddler, in that space of chaos and insanity between the ages of two and three, we were out one day running errands. I knew I was cutting it close to making one stop too many, but I did it anyway. When one has gone through the trouble of dressing their toddler for public scrutiny (socks *and* shoes), and dragged them 30 minutes from home, one wants to make the most of it.

After my last stop, tired and ready for an afternoon coffee or nap, I tried to get him into his car seat. He was *not* having it. He starfished, arms and legs flailing like a cat going to the vet.

As he melted down in an overtired puddle on the pavement outside the side door of my car, and I made apologetic "what can you do" faces to passersby, I tried to explain that we were finally going home.

I probably wasn't as patient as I'd hope to be. I, too, was overtired, hangry, and now frustrated. We were both at a low point, and I was *this close* to shoving that boy into that car with brute force just to be done with it. Tears be damned.

Instead, I made a choice that changed everything including how I parented from that moment on.

I asked him if I could have a hug, because *I* really needed one. He stopped screaming, his face crumpling with relief, and all but threw himself into my arms, and we sat there, in the Kmart parking lot, the tears flowing until we were both calmer.

Eventually he loosened his grip. I stood and held him, and told him how sorry I was. I was sorry I made that one last stop, and I should have known we were done, but I was ready to go home now, and I wanted some food. Did he want to get some food, too? He nodded. We got in the car. I smiled at him in the rearview mirror.

He fell asleep five minutes later.

I learned a valuable lesson that day, crouched outside the side door of my car, a wailing child in my arms: we are *all* toddlers when it comes to our emotions. I mean, yes, most of the time I can keep things under control and have the presence of mind to know when and where to express myself. I have a fully-formed prefrontal cortex now. But sometimes? When I am tired, hungry, sick, or overwhelmed, the big feelings of life become tsunamis that sweep me off my feet. And that's okay! In those moments, I don't need someone else to explain why my exhaustion is a result of my own poor life choices or that I should remember to pack snacks; those things aren't helpful when I'm melting down inside or out. When I'm at the end of my rope and figuratively or literally crying, the thing I need most is the simplest thing to give—a hug.

It is almost impossible to be angry, to feel alone, or to remain overwhelmed when I am hugging someone, *really* hugging them. (None of this pat-pat, there-there stuff. Lean into it. Let your bones go a little limp. Grip firmly for as long as you need. Push past any awkwardness and get to the good stuff.)

Toddlers have a lot to teach us, but the lesson my son taught me that day was that we all have big feelings, and the best antidote, the best way to bring those overwhelming feelings of not being able to deal is to seek out *connection.* My default was often to insist I could fix things myself, that somehow powering through, head down, without having to work with or through someone else was the easiest path forward. How mistaken I was.

Sometimes we can seek out that connection when we need it and ask for that hug, and, sometimes, we need outside help.

Years ago, my sister and I were holiday shopping at the mall in one of those stores with random meme-type mugs, joke gifts, and as it happened, an ear-piercing station. There was Christmas music blaring, the hum and chatter of groups of shoppers… and a sobbing four-year-old.

This child had just gotten an ear pierced and as anyone who has experienced this process knows, it hurts! The man this child was with was trying to convince her to get the second ear pierced, and much like the story of my sobbing toddler, this little girl was not having it.

The more the man tried to talk her into completing the process, the more this child rebelled. The more she cried and said "no!", the more frustrated he became. *You wanted to get this done*, he said. *I've already paid for two ears. You told your mom you were going to be brave. Just do it and let's be done with it. It can't hurt that much. Stop crying. You're being a baby.*

As the two spiraled, the child crying louder, the man beginning to yell at the child, I looked over to see the shop assistant trying to console the weeping child while shooting daggers of disapproval at the man.

By this point other customers had taken notice of what was happening, grumbling and mumbling amongst ourselves at how badly this man was handling things, and I did something entirely uncharacteristic for me. I intervened.

You might think I addressed the grown man's behavior as he was the adult here, and every frustrated word out of his mouth only made the child cry more intensely, but I didn't. The man, it was clear, needed a moment to collect himself. So, I nodded to him, stepped between him and the little girl, knelt down in front of her, and said a soft "hi."

I asked the shop assistant for a tissue and handed it to the little girl. I told her my name, showed her my ear piercings, and said I understood that getting your ears pierced can hurt at first and that that can be a surprise. She nodded, as her experience and tears were validated. I asked how old she was. She held up four fingers. I asked if she liked my earrings. She nodded. I complimented her on the choice she'd made for the earring she had in. As we chatted, she calmed down. I said that no one was going to make her get the second piercing and that that was up to her. What did she want to do?

She decided she would do the other side but wanted to wait for her mom. I glanced at the man who nodded and said the mom should be coming by soon.

I stood and faced him.

He seemed calmer and looked embarrassed by his earlier behavior. He wasn't the dad but the mom's boyfriend, he explained, and had been trying to help while the mom got some gifts in secret, but things had spiraled. He knew he hadn't handled it well.

Just then the mom in question rushed through the shop doors, arms laden with bags, and hurried over when she saw everyone huddled around her little girl.

I explained that she'd been startled by the first piercing but that we had talked and she just wanted to wait until mom was near to do side two.

As I turned to leave, the man thanked me.

I told him I understood.

We all need a moment sometimes.

We all need a moment sometimes.

I've thought about that interaction a lot over the years. I don't even remember now whether I was a mother at that point. What I was was a fellow human—able to understand both the pain and uncertainty of the child and the frustration and embarrassment of the man. He knew he was being judged for the little girl crying. He felt embarrassment for the situation getting out of hand, and also anger at the child for causing a scene. It devolved from there, and while I was at first another judgment-filled shopper shooting him daggers of annoyance for not controlling his temper, as I saw the dynamics of the situation, I realized that what he needed was a time-out. They both needed to pause, take a breath, and to be heard. This was his girlfriend's daughter. He didn't have parenting experience, was overwhelmed, and didn't want the girlfriend to be disappointed that he hadn't completed the task he'd assured her he could handle.

It makes me wonder how many times in our lives we try to power through a situation that is unraveling, spinning out of our control, our emotions bubbling over and out in ways we don't mean them to, only because we haven't been taught how to stop, pause, and take a breath.

I'm here to tell you: It's okay to take a breath.

Even if someone is waiting for us to carry on with their day. Even if they want us to get out of their way, because they are in a hurry to get to the front of the line or reach their destination. Even if it means that others will see us pausing and questioning our course or decisions so they'll know we aren't as sure-footed, in control, or confident as we'd like to project. It's okay to take a breath.

It's okay to take *two* breaths, or three, or enough to stop crying inside or hiccupping, enough time to allow our fists to unclench and our jaws to relax. It's okay to admit that our emotions have run riot over our calm and that our humanness is showing and that—no—we're not okay.

Because it's the admitting we're human, it's the taking of breaths, it's the seeing one another's humanness that allows us to find calm again. So, never feel that your only option is to yell at a child or act out when what you really need is to say, "Hey. Can I have a few minutes?" Or, "I need help." Give yourself the grace to be human, and give the humans around you the chance to be grace-filled and gracious.

## TIME-OUT IS A TOOL FOR EVERYONE

Speaking of time-outs, I have a confession. I hid in my room a lot as a parent. Or sometimes the bathroom. I don't feel proud of this truth, but I feel it doesn't get recognized enough: parenting is *hard.* And one of the hardest parts of parenting is controlling our emotions when we are also physically exhausted, overworked, and stressed which is probably 98% of parenthood.

Emotional regulation isn't something we talk a lot about as society except to allow men "anger" whereas others are expected to "swallow" their big feelings with cartons of ice cream or comically large wine glasses. Neither is a sustainable method of emotional regulation, but with our only answers given by society being humor and impractical soft skills, it's no wonder parents feel overwhelmed so much of the time.

When we are a parent to a neurodivergent kid or simply one whose personality challenges ours (I see you introverted parents of extroverted offspring and vice versa!), it's okay to acknowledge that, hey, as the parent, we might struggle sometimes or a lot of times.

It won't shatter your toddler's world to hear that "Mommy is feeling overwhelmed by how much mess there is in this room. Do you want to pick up before or after your nap?"

Imagine a world where we talk about our feelings instead of acting them out? Imagine a world where we build the skills of empathy, compassion, and self-care. Imagine a world attuned to the needs and emotions of others.

## PARENTING STYLES AND PITFALLS

We were in a rush to get to music class, the minutes tight as usual, and I asked my pre-school-aged son to wipe his chair seat clean of the food he'd dropped. "If someone else comes along and doesn't see it they will not like sitting on it."

A fellow mom rolled her eyes at me. "Why do you always give a reason? He should do it just because you said so."

*Just because I said so.*

I have often wondered in the years since that exchange how many of us have grown up in households where the reason we were expected to obey a command or comply with a request was nothing more compelling than that the person asking held authority over us. "Because I said so" isn't a reason; it's an expectation. It doesn't provide a lesson in critical thinking, decision making, or societal norms beyond obeying the hierarchies of patriarchy, class, age, and, to be harshly honest, racism.

Why should this person be respected or obeyed? Is it because they are older or in a position of authority? Is it because they are physically bigger or stronger?

That, by the way, is how abusers take advantage of those in their power.

What happens when the "child" is no longer smaller, weaker and doesn't feel like obeying? I distinctly remember my father recounting his own upbringing. When his mother deemed them in need of punishment for any infraction, she would take out the wooden ruler, have them come to her and tell them to open their palm for a sharp and painful thwack of the ruler. This form of punishment continued until my father was about twelve, and when she went to slap his palm, he grasped the ruler instead. "Because I said so" is only as effective as long as one has influence. Respect endures, not because of social or familial hierarchy, but because it is earned through actions which show consideration for others.

I knew then, as we were hurrying to clean up after our pizza lunch to get to music class, what the ensuing years have borne out: I wasn't showing weakness when explaining my request to my son. I was showing him that I have valid reasons behind every request and instruction and that my actions aren't random. I was imparting knowledge of how the world and our bodies work. I was inviting him, also, to seek context and to think about and understand the impact of his choices on himself and others. I was also teaching him that, because my asks aren't arbitrary, he could have faith that when I *didn't* provide a reason, I still had one, and it would be best to listen which is helpful when the situation required tact or urgency.

We don't leave food behind for others to sit on, because in a world where we have sat on food and stained our favorite item of clothing or touched something unpleasant, we wish someone had cleaned up after themselves. We don't eat all the available candy in one sitting, because when we are warned that we will get a tummy ache and then go behind our mother's back and sneak-eat all the cherry cordials, we find out that she was right. And when mom asks us to not speak, it's because she wants to spare someone's feelings or keep a happy surprise a surprise.

So, the next time a child in your life plays the "why?" game, see how long you can continue to provide thoughtful answers. You will be providing insight into your values, how adults navigate the endless decision making that goes into every moment of every day, as well as provide an opportunity for the child to see that sometimes, too, we don't have all the answers. And that, in itself, is a lesson.

## TRUST YOUR GUT

Back when our eldest was about six, we were homeschooling, so I didn't have an outside, experienced teacher noticing anything remarkable about his behavior compared to his peers. But one day I was leaving the grocery store, and I realized I was holding my 6-year-old's hand more tightly than my 3-year-old's, and something about that revelation gave me pause.

"I am worried he might have ADHD," I said to his pediatrician at our next visit. Our doc listened and asked a series of questions and we reviewed a diagnostic list together. As we went down the list, I knew our son who was bright and friendly, was also easily overwhelmed by too many steps to follow, forgetful, and impulsive.

I will always be grateful for what our doc said next: "I usually wait until we have corroborating evidence from the school before making a diagnosis, but the truth is, you know your child better than anyone."

---

*You know your child better than anyone.*
*You are the "expert" on your child.*

---

Who spends the most time with your child? Who understands how your child communicates their joys, their fears, how they behave when they are feeling unwell? Yes, healthcare professionals are trained in general, but a child's parents and primary caregivers have valuable insights into that specific child. Remember this when you need to advocate on behalf of your child.

I'll never forget the time when our son was but two years old and I came home from work to see him laying on our sofa. This normally highly active toddler didn't even get up to greet me. I went over to sit with him, brushed his hair back, and said to my husband, "We need to go to the ER."

"It's just a cold," my husband said. "He'll be fine with rest."

"He's breathing very shallowly," I said.

We debated this for a minute before I insisted, "We're going."

Our son was diagnosed with RSV. We were in the ER with him until the wee hours of the morning with him receiving nebulizer treatments and oxygen.

This is to say, trust your gut. Always. You are your child's advocate when they can't advocate for themselves. Your intuition could literally save your child's life.

I'm not going to say it's universal, but by listening to our own intuition we also build the muscle of tuning into our child, and that can help identify mental or emotional health issues down the road.

## WORK BUILDS CHARACTER

This is my hot take: having your child take a job as a teen is an important step in maturing and fostering responsibility, accountability, and a healthy work ethic. If you own a family business, it's fine to have your child work under someone else's direction, but it's better to have them apply for a weekend, summer, or part-time job where you aren't their boss.

Our kids both took on outside jobs during high school, and while neither loved getting up for work on weekends, dealing with unreasonable customers, or navigating the moods of coworkers and managers, that's kind of the point. Yes, it's great to earn some extra cash to have your own spending money or to tuck away for college or a car, but no entry-level job will make anyone rich. The value of work is in understanding that every cashier or laborer we will meet in this life deserves respect and is trying to make it through their day without drama. Entry-level or "menial" jobs expose us to people who have led difficult lives, are starting over after addiction or divorce, or who put their dreams on a shelf for various reasons. We will also see those who choose to greet each day with purpose and positivity and who want to help others succeed. These early jobs help us learn, before it counts on our career's resume, what it takes to be a valued coworker, a skilled manager, a problem-solver. We will know the kind of person we want to be seen as and the reputation we don't want to have. All for minimum wage.

There is value in hard work whether it is for a paycheck, personal enrichment, or charitable causes, so encourage your teen to set goals and engage in their community. Better yet, set the example of doing so, and we will all be richer for it.

## BE A JUDGMENT-FREE ZONE

When our teens reach the age where they could be tried as an adult in a court of law, legally married, or allowed to emancipate themselves, life is already prepared to bring down some pretty harsh consequences if they step out of line. Do we, as the parent, want to be another hammer of judgment ready to swing down on their head or the lifeline they reach for when they're overwhelmed and don't know where else to turn?

Yes, teens can be obstinate. They might talk back more than listen. They might seem hell-bent on frying our last nerve. But the truth is, in a very short time, they will be legally on their own and we won't be responsible for them but we will also not have influence—unless we foster that now.

Hopefully, we've been showing them in a thousand different ways that we love them unconditionally. That's never so important as the teen years. When that romantic connection turns sideways and they need an adult to extricate themselves, when the party gets out of hand, when they need a ride home or an escape plan that saves them face but also *saves them*, we have hopefully already made it clear that we are there for them. We might tell them in advance if they go out and have too much to drink or whatever, that we will pick them up, no questions asked. As their judgment-free zone, we can let them experience natural consequences while also knowing that someone out there has their back when everything falls apart.

Our teens are learning how to be adults. Rather than make those lessons harsh, allow those lessons to feel like a close call they survived. Because if they don't have us to call on? They or their friends might not survive their choices.

I'd rather bail my kid out of jail, drive them to rehab, or file a restraining order on their behalf, than attend their funeral.

It's okay to be disappointed *and* loving. It's okay to want our kids to listen, dang it, so they can avoid hard and traumatizing experiences. Some parents tell themselves that "all teens go through a rebellious stage" or "boys will be boys," and wash their hands of both impact and responsibility. It is a harder job sitting in the discomfort of knowing every kid is likely to begin walking a path they later regret starting. I can tell you it's a relief to get that call knowing you have the opportunity to guide them back to safety.

And if you didn't have that adult in your life? I'm so sorry. I hope that when it comes to your own children, you are able to be the parent you wanted in those moments.

## TRANSITIONING TO MENTOR – HOW TO PARENT YOUR ADULT CHILD

When our first-born left for college, I prepared myself for the waves of grief everyone so caringly warned about in the hushed tones usually reserved for discussing terminal illness and death. I packed tissues and braced myself for move-in day. I had best friends on stand-by for those first empty nesting weeks. I waited for the sobbing to begin. I'm a weeper. Surely the tears were only a matter of time.

But at drop-off, while I admit to feeling momentarily nostalgic (as I discreetly palmed a tissue to my husband), my overwhelming feelings were those of excitement for our son and relief that we'd somehow managed to get this wonderful, messy, brilliant, scattered, lovable child launched into the world. I high-fived hubby on the way home and life went on.

Four years later–after celebrating kid #1's diploma and kid #2's high school graduation– it was our youngest's turn to spread their wings.

The warnings about our soon-to-be empty nest had been rumbling like thunder in the distance since June. As such, I'd spent the summer in a flurry of distracting activities buying dorm supplies and ironing out logistical issues, like a hurricane prepper hoarding plywood. Maybe everyone was right? Maybe this time, when my baby left the nest, it would hit different?

I delivered them to their dorm one Sunday in sweltering heat, making a glorious impression, I'm sure, on all the other parents, delicate rivers of sweat soaking my mask and my hair declaring war in the humidity. The perky RA came by repeatedly to offer lunch at the dining hall as if anyone moving mini-fridges in 90 degree heat wanted anything but a full-body dunk in an ice bath.

Giving my kid one last squeezy hug, I hopped in the car. I felt myself well up a bit as I scrounged for wet wipes with which to bathe, waved goodbye to my baby–the child who I could swear just yesterday I caught coming into the world–and drove away.

And that was it.

I drove five hours sipping the iced tea I got at the drive through, scrolling through radio stations, playing with the cruise control of my car–not crying, not feeling bereft, looking forward to a shower, hoping my kiddo was settling in well.

Monday morning I woke up with the dogs too early for my liking, fed the cats, waved goodbye to hubby on his way to work and took stock. I decided maybe I needed to give things a few days. Surely I was in shock and the grief had yet to set in. I made fresh coffee.

Then Wednesday arrived.

And nothing.

Don't get me wrong. I love my children with a ferocity and pride I can't quite describe, but they were never mine to keep. Our job these many years was to shepherd them through childhood in one piece, give them the tools and lessons and support they needed to go out into the world and do their thing. Remember how it felt to launch into the world? Remember that? I do. Home felt like the clothes I was outgrowing on the way to adulthood.

Remember, too, how exciting it was to buy and choose new clothes?

That's the excitement I felt for my kids as they embarked on their new adventures. They would decide what they liked, how they wanted to be in this world, and that's fun and a space of dreams and possibilities. I never wanted to be the cord that held my kids back, just the soft place for them to land should they need it.

Our house is emptier and quieter when they aren't home, a bit like being left standing in the aftermath of a storm that's been swirling in our lives for two decades. I remember in those first days of after college drop-offs, putting things away and to rights, tucking away those items left scattered in the final mad dash to pack, the storm of youth at their backs…

We're still here, my husband and I, the survivors, surveying the changed landscape of our lives. Remembering the tree that used to be out front with the fairy houses underneath, the sandbox that's now overgrown and being reclaimed by the neighboring woods. I walk around this house and remember who and what my husband and I dreamed about before the storms of parenthood blew them off course and took us in new directions.

Then I set about cleaning. Getting things in order. Planning new plans. Writing. I feel blessed that my husband and I can look at one another, recognize one another despite the weathering of the years, and still genuinely like one another. It's okay if we cry. It's okay if we don't. Parenthood is messy and disorienting. Those of us who've reached the empty nest phase of life should be proud to have made it through the storm.

As for me?

I always look forward to hearing tales of high winds and cleansing rains when my little birds fly back for a visit, because my kids are now out in the world living life and dreaming dreams, and that's exactly how it should be.

Parenting is all about building a relationship with that child. As a parent we are their advocate and caregiver. As they grow, we are the guardrails of safety but also someone who has "been there and done that." We as parents provide insights into how to navigate life, self-expression and hormonally-impacted emotions. Eventually, for most of us, the expectation is that this growing person will evolve into a functioning adult and member of society. But for many, that is a *rough* transition.

It has been my limited experience that when a parent steps back from imposing rigid rules or limits, a teen has nothing to rebel against. If the expectation of having to experience the natural consequences of one's actions is established in earlier, impressionable years, our teens will already be in the habit of not thinking about what *we* might do but *what might happen.* It's a subtle difference, but it is the difference between our teens seeing us as the opposition versus on their side.

We talked early and often to our kids in their growing years about choices other people made and whether they would have made those choices. It helped them to see all sides of a behavior or action and to think beyond the moment. This isn't to say my kids were angels who never hid anything from their parents (as the

Halloween candy wrappers under the mattress would attest), but neither were they oppositional or chronically rebellious.

I was recently texting with a friend whose adult child had moved across the country. I shared that my own adult child was talking about applying to schools abroad, and how I had needed to take a breath before saying, "You don't need it, but you have my permission to go wherever your heart leads you."

It's hard being a parent, maybe especially if we enjoy a good relationship with our child. Our whole job is to prepare our child to go out into the world with the inner strength and resources to follow their dreams and tackle life's challenges—without us there to immediately catch them if they stumble. One of the hardest moments of parenthood is to have that kite string pulled taught… and then to let go of it.

I know I have to let go of it, because that child was never mine to keep. That child has their own destiny and life's purpose, hopes, dreams, and desires. They have free will, and children who find themselves bound by that parental kite string will grow to resent it, even cut it themselves.

But letting go of the end of the string frees both of us. Now, as much as I will remain available for whenever my child decides to swoop down into my life for a brief moment or longer visit, whether the storms of life ground them for a time or whether they are simply showing me the joy of flying. I will make myself available as they need me, but I am not responsible for their flight or path.

## WHEN CHILDREN VEER OFF COURSE

Should my kite-child choose to dip down into the sea or fly well beyond where I can retrieve them, that, too, is up to them, and not for me to feel at fault for any hardship that may befall them.

Because as many times as I've been told I have good kids and I've done a good job, I know that a good portion of that is up to chance. As much as we can do things "right" as parents, there's a whole lot that isn't in our control. Mental illness. Addiction. Poor life choices. Risk-taking behavior. The negative impact of other adults in our children's lives. As adults, our children may do things we don't like, don't agree with, or outright disapprove of, and there's a difference between being supportive and loving and enabling or feeling responsible for someone else. As parents it is our job to model the behaviors we want to see and to apologize and make amends when we don't live up to that mark. In this way, we release ourselves from judgment while holding ourselves accountable.

We may not always like our children's actions, but we should strive to always love them enough to free them to make their own choices as well as hold them accountable for the impacts of those choices.

---

*As a parent, I am responsible for my own actions.*
*I need to let go of the string.*

*When my child is an adult, they are free and*
*therefore responsible for their own actions.*

---

Still, if you're in that moment of letting go of that kite string? Big hugs to you. Big hugs. Uncurl your fingers, each and every one, as you had done for you or wish your own parents had done. There. You did it. Big hugs.

## WHEN OUR PARENTS FAILED US

It never fails that in a discussion about parenting someone will pipe up and say, "Well, my parents smacked me around and I turned out okay!"

I'm so sorry to tell you, that you are not, in fact, "okay". You are wounded, defiant, and I'm guessing that those who speak these "truths" the loudest have repeated those behaviors with their own children and now feel, deep down, that they wished they'd made different choices.

I gently and with utmost compassion feel compelled to tell you: you are not "okay." You survived the experience. You survived. But that behavior that left you feeling helpless, isolated, shamed, or alone didn't teach you anything good about other humans or adults. It didn't teach you how to regulate your emotions, or modulate your impulses. It didn't teach you nuance, grace, forgiveness, emotional regulation, how to make amends or give a heartfelt apology. The "shut ups" and punitive time-outs and threats of physical harm, didn't toughen you for the real world, they made walls behind which you later isolated and protected yourself emotionally. They left you with shame you turned on yourself or swallowed with food or alcohol. They made you defiant and reckless and rebellious, but they did not leave you "okay."

It's not your fault, though. It was never your fault. Your parents, too, probably suffered their own traumas, and that cycle may well have been going on for generations.

Maybe it's too late. Maybe you have already repeated the lessons you were taught, but it's never too late to say, "I'm sorry." It's never too late to say, "You didn't deserve that." It's never too late to speak to your own childhood self and say, "I'm so sorry that happened. You didn't deserve that. You were just a child."

Sit with that for a moment. Instead of insisting that you're okay, recognize that *not* being okay about those things is valid. You are allowed to feel your real feelings! Your parents were adults, they were responsible for governing themselves, and they may have failed you.

Imagine giving your younger self a hug. Be the adult you wish had been there for you to help you navigate the space that felt too large, too scary, too violent, or too angry to cope with at the time. Allow your younger self to be vulnerable with adult you, because you? *You have the power to make your own safe space.*

Parents should, ideally, raise their children with unconditional love. If you were made to feel you had to jump through certain hoops or walk on eggshells or face the wrath of a parent, if they withheld affection unless you behaved a certain way, that's conditional. That's transactional. That is not the unconditional love which is every human's birthright.

Even good parents misstep, make mistakes, and have moments they wish they could rewrite. It's okay to admit that your parent, whom you might still have love for, hurt you or didn't see when you were hurting. It's okay to not be okay and it's okay to forgive or not forgive, but don't lie to yourself. You—and especially younger you—deserve the truth.

## A SOFT PLACE TO LAND

Unconditional love, on the other hand, is something none of us will ever outgrow. As our children grow into young adults and we transition to the role of mentor, moving from the one who actively guides to the one who stands ready to offer advice or wisdom, we are providing a model of supportive care which will take us through to when our roles may well reverse.

My son is a young adult now. He's navigated through schooling, an advanced degree, a job search, roommates, his first jobs and love. He knows now that not everyone out there enjoys the reassurance we have been lucky enough to provide him and that is the knowledge that he can take risks in life knowing that no matter what happens, his father and I will be here to the best of our ability to provide a soft place to land. We will ensure that if that job doesn't pan out or his heart gets broken or he changes his mind about a course of study or career, that we are here to provide shelter, food, and emotional comfort until such time as he is ready to venture out into the world again.

Too many children of any age don't have that cushion. Their parents might be unwilling or not financially or emotionally secure themselves. Perhaps they are of the "I supported you until you were 18 and now you are on your own" school of thought.

Anyone can be a soft place to land, though. As our son's girlfriend, who doesn't enjoy the same relationship with her parents, struggled to make a decision about her future, I took her to lunch and told her this: "Independent of your relationship with my son, I want you to know that we are here to support you. Please make your decision knowing that whatever happens, we will not let you go without food, shelter, and a place to call home. I want you to feel free to come to me whenever you feel the need."

Knowing we have a safety net available allows us to make decisions for our own highest good. It frees us from choosing soul-crushing careers that "pay the bills" or remaining in relationships that are toxic or have stagnated because we have "nowhere else to go." These soft places to land don't have to be with biological family, either. We can create chosen family groups or communities that give us the reassurance that no matter how life's storms might treat us, we will always have a place to be cared for, a place to regroup, and a place that will build us up again.

## WHEN PARENTHOOD IS NOT FOR US

Parenthood is such a large part of the human experience for so many of us, we may sometimes forget it's not universal, so I want to take a moment to speak to those who have either intentionally chosen to remain childless or for whom circumstance has chosen for them.

To those with uteri who choose not to bear children, I see you. I see your humanness. Your awareness of your own goals or limits. I see that you have looked at your life, your circumstances, your partner, your responsibilities, your resources, your physical body, and your dreams and made the conscious decision to exist in this life with authenticity. I honor and respect your choice as should those around you. I wish you much happiness and opportunities to nurture and mentor in ways that speak to your soul. It is neither selfish nor amoral to choose such a path.

For those for whom parenthood was or is a dream circumstances have prevented from coming to fruition, I see you, too. I hold you with tenderness in my heart. I want you to know that I also see the nurturing, loving, guiding parts of you seeking to be made manifest, and I want to tell you that those pieces of you that yearn to grow cannot be stunted by circumstance. They will only be transformed. No, it is not the same to be a beloved auntie. It is not the same to be a foster parent, become a big brother/sister, mentor youth at your religious organization, teach others wherever you may find yourself, or nurse/nurture/feed/assist others in the thousand different ways that exist in our world. None of it is the same. I will not claim it to be, and you are justified in mourning the loss of the future you'd hoped for—for yourself, your partner, and your potential children.

We all grieve something in this lifetime, and this particular grief is yours to carry, process, and come to terms with. I am so sorry.

But I will also not accept that your identity as nurturer, teacher, or caregiver is forfeited, and neither should you.

Human children are the common recipients of parenting, but so are fur-children, extended family, and children whose families cannot or will not provide the safe haven and loving care we who love humanity would want for all children.

Please take the time to grieve for what isn't and what will not be, and when you are ready, I hope you open that generous heart of yours to the possibilities that still exist to love unconditionally. Because that? That is what we most need in this world. *You.*

PART 5

# EDUCATION

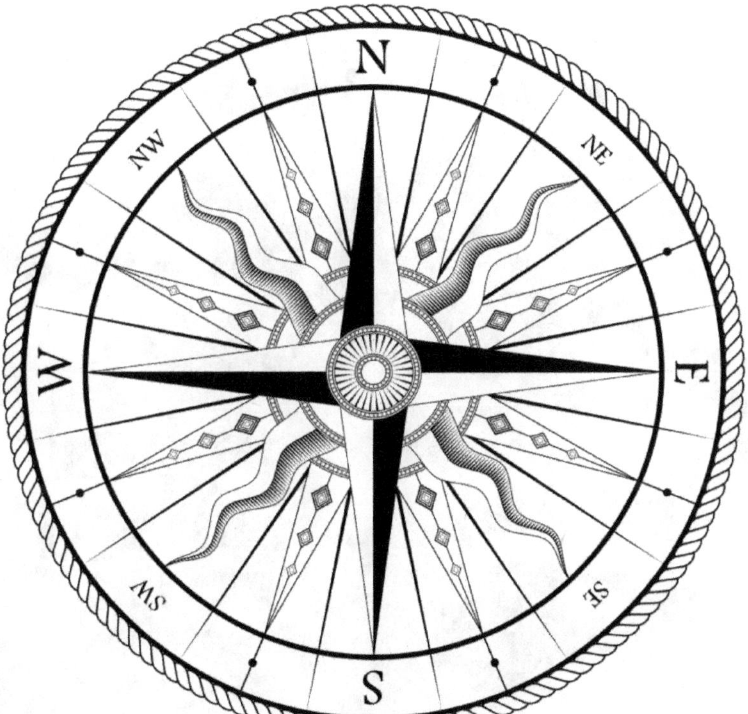

# Chapter 8

## EDUCATION

### LEARNING IS A LIFETIME ADVENTURE

---

*The day I stop learning is the day I die.*

---

Those are strong words and a bit foreboding, but for me they are not simply a call to action, a seeking of knowledge but a willingness to be open to new information, ideas, and perspectives. Too often, it seems, aging comes with a sort of mental paralysis. The way we've done things becomes the way we've *always* done the things, and soon we can't conceive of anyone ever doing anything differently. But that mindset is so, so limiting!

I prefer to challenge myself to do my little puzzle games each evening, to actively engage in deep conversation with people younger than me, and to meet each day with a sense of curiosity.

Think about it. If we ever come to a point where we feel we've seen it all and know it all, what is the point of going through the motions of life without the living piece of it? Sure, perhaps we've gained some useful experiences and perspective and that's valuable to share, but like the scientific method, we should come up with hypotheses, test them, come to conclusions and then *be open to new information.* If I think of myself as one human science experiment in biology and sociology and spirituality and what have you, then I am always comparing what I've already learned to the new information and data that is always there to be discovered.

This openness to possibility of what our future can hold is particularly important for those of us going through major life transitions. When our young adults go off to college or move out or we approach retirement, we may wonder what is next for us.

Let yourself wonder. Lean into all the possibilities to chase after old hobbies or interests you hadn't made time for before. In his "retirement" my husband has taken up an interest in sailing. He continues volunteering for underprivileged youth seeking higher education. He sings in choral ensembles. We do home renovation projects. We have traveled. I continue to write.

These transition times are a chance to write our next chapter. Choose the fancy pens. Open the crisp new notebooks. Get writing!

## LEARNING STYLES & PHILOSOPHIES OF LEARNING

I am a kinesthetic learner. Do not tell me how to do something or show me a video or diagram and expect me to toddle off and perform the task. If my body is not doing the thing I'm trying to learn, physically going through the motions of the task, I struggle to absorb that information. So how in heaven's name did I manage to succeed in classes which used lectures and books to teach me things?

I took copious notes.

You see, the very action of moving a pen on paper triggered the parts of my brain that absorbed information. My notes were messy, largely unorganized except for occasional arrows or stars or underlines for major points. I rarely reviewed them. But despite hours-long lectures in college, I was able to absorb information and succeed because I had learned how *I* learn.

Your learning style may well be different than mine. Perhaps you have a photographic memory and just need to see a picture or draw it out. Perhaps you need to hear information and so text to voice apps are your immediate friend. My point is, that learning and hurdles to learning (which we'll address later) are as individual as the learner, but if we pause for a moment and think about how we best absorb new information, we can use that as a tool for making learning easier and accessible.

The basic modes of taking in new information are: visual, auditory, read/write, and kinesthetic. If you struggle to absorb information for a class or in work meetings, think about which is your preferred learning style and see if there is a way to adapt your inputs. This is also a helpful exercise to use with children. Successful students have learned how to learn. Let me say that again:

---

*Successful students have learned how to learn.*

---

My son is also a kinesthetic learner. How did we learn and memorize the times tables? Jumping jacks. Drumming. I had this energetic boy actively learn by keeping him active while learning. We used rolling dice to do math exercises. We used his auditory learning mode by quizzing math facts at random. *(What's 12 times 4? Divided by 2? Plus 7?)*

My daughter is a visual learner. She needs silence to learn and prefers to read/write. When she was little and I asked her what she wanted for breakfast she would hold up a finger, run for pen and paper, and draw a picture of a cereal bowl. I know that when she's studying, she needs it pin-drop quiet.

Yes, homeschooling them when they were young was a challenge for obvious reasons, but ultimately both were successful students in the long run, because we identified what environments and modalities made learning easier for them.

## RAISING KIDS WHO LOVE LEARNING

One of the lessons I learned as a parent was that learning is not always linear. Watching a child develop different skills as they grow proves this, as we can witness language leapfrogging hand-eye coordination which might toggle on and off with advancements in reading social cues. We as parents accept this non-linear pace for developmental milestones but often forget the same is true for academics.

I had the privilege of being able to homeschool my kids in their elementary years. My son through junior high and my daughter through second grade. Homeschooling is not for everyone, not for every family or every child and you may well have a visceral reaction to my choice. Without going too deep into our reasons, my son had some significant food sensitivities when he was younger that we struggled to control when he was out and about in the world. We had a friend group of like-minded, involved parents with similarly-aged kids, and we began our journey putting together a collaborative pre-school group that met each week at a different house. It evolved from there. As we tapped into the local homeschool community, we met parents whose philosophy ran everywhere from unschooling to strict biblically-based curricula. We chose an a la carte version of practical and workbook-style lessons along standard subject areas, but we also allowed for student-led learning where, if our child wasn't feeling up to an hour of reading practice, that's okay! We'll work ahead in math.

Both of my kids, as a result, were allowed the flexibility to learn subjects at the pace they were ready for in an environment that worked for them and via their preferred learning modality. In traditional schools, they would have been deemed slow and/or delayed readers, and as the children of an author and avid reader I often struggled to be at peace with the process.

Fast forward a bit, and I realized that my black/white, tell-me-the-rule-and-let-there-be-no-exceptions son struggled with the vagaries of spelling and pronunciation in our written language. Once he overcame that hurdle, he went straight to books about facts. No fiction for him for the longest time. Our daughter? Once she "got" reading, it was as if an entire world opened to her. She won the second-grade summer reading contest by a country mile, would take tote bags to the library and assured the librarian that, yes, she definitely was going to read that entire stack of books that week, immersed herself in fictional worlds, and gleefully re-read favorites again and again.

They both graduated from college with highest honors in wildly unrelated fields, but the common denominator is that they each approached learning with a curiosity fostered and rooted in being allowed to pursue their intellectual interests at their own pace.

This is all a very long-winded way of saying that if you are an adult who "hated" school and have strong feelings about "book learning", I hope you will find a way to spark and feed your curiosity. Maybe you are already doing so without naming it as "learning" and that's okay! If you go down rabbit holes of interest, or belong to a club of any sort, I guarantee you are still learning. Lean into that, you amazing human, you!

Learning is simply curiosity with intent. Curiosity can exist on its own, but give it a goal? Oh, the places you'll go!

## RAISING KIND KIDS WITH COMMON SENSE

We've all seen and heard the adage about ivory-tower academics who lack common sense and practical skills. It's a trope that is often used to defend those for whom the educational system didn't address or meet our learning style or didn't adapt to a learning hurdle we might have had. That old saying is also pointing out that reading a philosophy text isn't going to help a person change a tire or realize they ought not to leave a can of soda in their car in below zero temperatures. So how do we raise kids who both value intellectual curiosity *and* give them the practical skills to navigate their world without others shaking their heads?

First of all, you don't. Common sense and practical skills are gained in two ways: observation and experience. We either watch someone change a tire or we are on the side of the road, bereft of cell signal, with a jack and a need to get somewhere. Every person will have holes in their experience or knowledge base, and it's unfair to judge the "common sense" skills of someone raised in downtown Manhattan to those raised in rural anywhere. Their lived experiences are different, but plunk that farm-raised person in the subway system and see how quickly their derision turns to dismay.

So, let's hit pause for a minute on which "common sense" skills are more practical or useful and think a bit about what it takes to raise a child who is emotionally aware and adaptable, because that's really what we're looking for. We model kindness in order to raise kind children. That's it. I have no further notes. If we want our kids to be attuned to the needs and feelings of others, the easiest way to teach that is to be attuned to our children's needs and feelings and those around us. Be the people we want them to become.

Adaptability is another animal. If my child is plunked down into an unfamiliar environment, what are the tools and resources they'll need to navigate this safely and effectively?

---

*Natural consequences are the quickest way to learn something.*

---

Obviously, I didn't leave my kids to fend for themselves without guidance or guardrails in a jungle to teach them survival skills, but within the space of "this is ill-advised but not going to cause lasting harm" I allowed them to experience the natural consequences of their actions if my words of caution weren't being heeded. Perhaps they got colder than they would have because they allowed their mittens to get wet. Perhaps they got a tummy ache by eating more of the thing I advised them against eating more of. You get the idea. By allowing my kids to experience some of the less fun things in life, I gave them an opportunity to begin to build their own decision-making skills. Do I want to see how deep that puddle is? When I stepped in it last time I got water in my shoe. This time I will use a stick!

## DON'T BE AFRAID TO MAKE MISTAKES

After my grandmother passed away, I inherited a set of four small porcelain plates. They are a lovely pattern with pink dogwood flowers, and so I bought plate hangers and displayed them in my dining room in a neat little row over the pass-through opening to our kitchen.

Our dining room is also a multi-functional space where a lot of family gatherings take place, and it so happened that we were gathering with our teen children when we opened a snowball fight kit.

I think you can see where this is going.

Apparently, a single dense pom-pom is hefty enough when hurled by a teenager to knock a small porcelain plate off its moorings and come crashing to the floor. My teens froze in horror as my grandmother's small plate shattered on impact and looked to me to gauge how I would react.

"Whoops," I said.

They were deeply apologetic, but the truth is, while I was sad that my perfect set of four was now a lop-sided set of three, it was an accident which happened while we were all living and laughing and loving. I assured them I could still fondly remember my grandmother with the three remaining plates and life went on.

Years later, my husband and I arrived home after a long trip. My eldest had been housesitting. As I walked in the door and looked at the place where my grandmother's plates hung, there was a new addition on the bare nail that had been empty for several years.

A small reindeer face looked back at me, a child's whimsical coat hook now hung on the fourth nail. Does this reindeer face match my dining room décor? No, it does not. Will I take that reindeer down? Never. That face reminds me that mistakes happen, but love and laughter are my favorite ways to decorate any room.

---

*Mistakes and accidents are a lesson in learning how to own our faults, make amends, and forgive ourselves and others.*

---

We all make mistakes. Every last one of us. Mistakes are an inevitable part of learning what works and what doesn't. But too many of us have at one point or another being punished for accidents that, yes, might have been somewhat foreseeable, but due to a lack of attention or experience or just the distractions of the moment, happened anyway. How we react to the inevitable accidents in life have an impact on whether those around us fear making mistakes near us or feel free to live life.

As a parent, I've seen how important it is to forgive mistakes with grace and understanding. Perhaps showing a mortified and apologetic new driver how to buff the scratches out of a car's bumper is a better lesson about checking and rechecking our side-view mirrors before backing up than screaming about responsibility and paying attention.

As the years go by, my kids have learned that mistakes happen, but that owning those mistakes and making amends is possible. Because they haven't been punished for being human and flawed, they are less fearful of trying new things and are more understanding when those around them aren't perfect.

I say all this not only to speak to the parents out there, but to the child in each of us who has made mistakes. I urge you to reframe those moments as forgivable even if they weren't treated that way in the moment. Think about how you'd behave, what you'd strive for, what you'd allow yourself to express interest in if you weren't afraid to make mistakes.

Too many of us had moments during our earlier years where we were afraid that a mistake meant we were doing learning wrong, and it made us associate learning with anxiety and feelings of inadequacy. To those for whom this resonates: the inadequacy was in the adults in that moment failing to find a way to reach you where you were. But it's not too late to reignite that spark and love for learning.

## REIGNITING THE SPARK—THERE IS NO TIMELINE

Like I said earlier in this chapter, the day I stop learning is the day I die, and while that may seem dramatic and hyperbolic, I believe it. What is the point of being here in this world if we feel we have won the game, reached the end, gotten all we're going to get out of it? Sure, we can write a book and pretend we know some things we've learned along the way, but if we aren't open to hearing what *else* there is, if we aren't open to refining our views or sharing our selves with those struggling or simply being curious about this amazing world and universe we live in, are we *living?*

I am a terrible gardener. I have a long history of killing houseplants. But this year, again, I'm trying to grow some veggies in some raised beds and reading about companion planting and natural pest-management, because I'm a human who likes fresh produce and so even though maybe I should have learned this by now, I haven't, and I'm not too proud to admit this is something I want to try to do.

I would love to learn to quilt. I've enjoyed archery, and my husband and I have talked about moving from tennis to pickle ball because people our age do that. My kids are learning foreign languages on their cell phones, my husband is going on a boat-building trip this summer, and my point is you can try new things or dig deeper into old hobbies and interests and online videos are just as valid as in-person classes for gaining knowledge. Maybe the skill or knowledge you have an interest in acquiring is a casual, "Hey, you want to sign up for this one-day thing with me?" invite to your partner or friend or even a treat to yourself. Learning has no timeline. It's the natural state for humans to learn. If you are feeling anti-intellectual, it's because someone worked to put out that spark in you.

You have the power to reignite that spark. If it means going back to school to earn a certificate or degree or to gain a skill, don't let anyone tell you that's frivolous, because that's literally what humans *do*.

## EMOTIONAL GROWTH, NEURO DIVERGENCE, AND MORE

At their child's first pediatric appointment and each annual visit, every parent is given the gift of anxiety in the form of a growth and milestone chart. Their child is compared to all the other children, and even when that child falls within the bounds of all children, the desire to have one's child exceed developmental milestones or fall within the middle of growth ignores the fact that every single one of us has likely fallen on the outskirts of a various measure at some point. Perhaps we were delayed in walking or fell at the tall end of our peers. As parents we are encouraged to obsess over and mark milestones in baby books and report them to healthcare providers. And, yes, being aware of how our child is doing compared to others can be useful in identifying issues to address before they grow into problems.

*But,* it's important to balance what we are told to expect with an acceptance of the natural diversity within human growth and development. Our son was "late" in terms of walking, but he climbed like a monkey, and had an outsized vocabulary by the age of two. He now has a career in Computer Science, neither an acrobat nor an orator. Our daughter was very quiet and reserved as a child. She was the observer, but she's also a leader in her university's Philosophy Club and Student Senate. Early growth is not always an indicator of later interests or abilities.

What if your child *does* have an issue with language, information processing, memory recall, hand-eye coordination, or any other number of common impediments to learning and navigating everyday life or traditional school environments? What then?

The measure of where someone falls on a chart might indicate a need for interventions or accommodations. We've navigated those waters. Trust me. But what I learned is that there is both challenge and opportunity when discovering your child falls outside the "norm."

Yes, my child wasn't like others, and we worked with various modalities and professionals to provide support and education to help our neurodivergent child navigate the world they lived in. You will, I'm sure, have your own sense of whether we did the right thing, but in looking back on those years, I'm glad we did the following:

1) We told our child they could view their neurodivergence as a superpower. Yes, it was overwhelming, but they saw the world in a way most of those around them didn't. They were capable of holding many ideas in their head at once and while overwhelming, this mass of ideas allowed them to make connections and think of solutions that others could not. Their experiences as a neurodivergent individual in this world have made them empathetic to others who may not fit the norm. As a team leader at work, they strive to see the unique skills each team member brings to the table and works to build a community for all.

2) We avoided language which framed our neuro-divergent child/self as too [fill in the blank]. Rather, they had an abundance of [fill in the blank].

3) We celebrated and encouraged their interests. All of them. For however long they held an interest until there were clear favorites. Allowing a child to feel success in an area they

are passionate about builds self-esteem and allows them to become an expert others will seek out despite any social awkwardness.

4) Their random passions and hyper-fixation may well be the key to their future. Lean into it. Feed it, but don't try to drive it. You've had your life to lead. Let them lead theirs with your support.

5) Be aware of sensitivities to sound, social gatherings, texture, etc. Their sensitivities are where you are being called to be a buffer for them as they grow. This isn't them being "too sensitive" any more than someone with a known allergy is being "difficult" for having their throat swell. We make accommodations for those we want to include. Why wouldn't we do that for our own children?

6) Scaffold until they can support themselves. We worked to get an IEP at school to ensure that teachers prompted our child to write down assignments and turn them in. We chose medications to aid with focus, because, as our pediatrician said, "We don't ask near-sighted students to go without glasses." For those children who need mobility aids, or therapy, or a service animal, or any number of other supportive or adaptive aids, we do this not because they are incapable of ever learning to exist without them but because it makes no sense to refuse to provide support while it's still needed. Tools are available in so many forms. Use them. Provide them. Advocate for them.

7) Finally, and maybe most importantly, allow your child to be exactly who they are. Let go of whatever expectations you

> had for their future and let them—in all their wonderful uniqueness—determine the future meant for them.

I freely admit there were days when our kid was struggling with emotional regulation and executive function and I wondered *how?* How is this child ever going to manage to become a self-sufficient and functioning adult? They sometimes forgot to put on shoes! If I could go back in time and reassure my former self, I would tell myself this: relax. It will be years until this child is fully cooked. Give them time. Give them love. They've learned so much up to this point. They will surely learn more in the years to come.

Back in my college days I worked as a peer tutor. One semester I was assigned a student who was struggling to pass his introductory accounting course. He was diagnosed with several learning disabilities and challenges including: ADHD, short-term memory processing, long-term memory recall, and test anxiety. When he came to me, he was on his way to failing the class. But his final grade? B+! How? We learned how he learned and made it a game. We used every modality we could to help him understand the game of accounting so that he understood the logic of why something was done so that he could, even if he couldn't remember the steps, recreate the how. Many of those tutoring sessions were me providing pep talks, learning why he wanted to take this class (he hoped to help in his father's business), and reassuring him that even though this wasn't easy for him, we would find a way. Most of all, he knew that I wasn't going to make fun of him or give up on him.

Education isn't about filling an empty vessel with information so that it can be upended on a test. That's simply information transfer. Education is, fundamentally, helping another human learn how they learn. It's giving someone the courage to follow their curiosity and the keys to unlock the treasure chests of knowledge out in this world. From there, the tests and the educator are superfluous. As they should be.

PART 6

# MONEY MATTERS

# Chapter 9

## MONEY MATTERS

### A TALE OF TWO FRIENDS

Many years ago, when our kids were little, my friend and I found ourselves bailing each other out. She covered me for our son's monthly piano lessons when I forgot my checkbook. A week later I paid for her share of a joint gift. Soon thereafter, she put in a combined order for Scholastic books, a week later I paid for lunch for all of us, and soon after brought her groceries and ginger ale when her family got trapped at home with the stomach flu.

This back and forth went on for months with each of us promising we were keeping track and would come up with the tally we owed one another when we found the time. Easily six months went by before I decided I had to pay her back. I took all my little notes to myself and sat down with my calculator and although the total we'd each paid on the other's behalf was over a hundred dollars, the amount I actually owed her was less than two dollars.

Months of back and forth and numerous transactions and the difference was less than the cost of a cup of coffee.

I used this anecdote often with my kids over the years, and while, yes, you absolutely don't want to be the one who is always on the hook for paying for things, in a truly equal friendship or partnership it's okay to let go of keeping track of the pennies and dimes in favor of being ready to be there for one another. When we are equally generous and there for one another, we will always come out whole.

In case you believe this is a one-off experience, I just reenacted this lesson with my son. Over the course of several months, I paid his share of a boat-building experience for later in the year. He bought a solar battery for us. I bought his girlfriend's birthday gift so she wouldn't see the box. He paid for two Costco runs and a pizza dinner. When I tallied everything we had paid—even though the total spent by each of us was over $1500?—I ended up owing him a grand total of: $13.47.

## HOW TO CHANGE YOUR RELATIONSHIP WITH MONEY

I've read reports that the top sources of conflict between couples are sex, money and kids.

I believe it. All of these affect us personally and are sources of disagreement on how much we should have, how we relate to it, and our experiences from the past.

But I'm talking about money here.

One of the most a-ha moments I have had in life was realizing that one's view of money as either a *useful tool* or *scarce resource* changes everything. Let me explain.

I was in a workshop some years ago discussing limiting beliefs, internal narratives or "truths" we accept that hold us back from achieving our goals or living free of anxiety. One of the exercises asked participants to write down a word or phrase that described how they felt about money. That was it. Write one word.

I wrote the word "useful". The woman beside me wrote "scarce".

The woman beside me had high anxiety relating to money. She never felt she had enough even when she had money in the bank, a roof over her head, food to eat, and clothes on her back. She had a car in which she drove to the workshop, but her view of money was that it was a scarce resource, one she needed to be sure to keep track of and over which she often worried whether she had enough.

When it got to me, I thought about the times in my life I had literally stood in the grocery store and debated between splurging on cheese or peanut butter, because I didn't have the budget for both. Half way through college, I remember having to call home and ask my dad to loan me funds for a security deposit so I could rent a room the next semester. I wasn't destitute, but I was aware that money wasn't falling from trees into my bank account.

But when it was my turn to share my word for money, I said, "Useful."

I don't see money as valuable in and of itself but as useful for what it can be exchanged for. I see it as a tool through which I gain access to food, shelter, etc. But in viewing it as a tool and not a resource in itself, my mind isn't in a scarcity mindset around it but in one of abundance and possibility. If at some point I didn't have access to the "tool" of money, then I would seek out other avenues to reach my goals.

I may be no more or less wealthy than someone who sees money as a limited resource, but because I am not focused on hoarding it, I have always somehow had enough, and I haven't had anxiety around it. Do I make a budget? Of course! Have I been caught short some months? Absolutely.

This is in no way meant to minimize the real issues of homelessness, food insecurity, and the like. Those are real and complex issues often tied to insufficient investment as a society in a universal minimum wage, mental health, affordable housing, etc., etc., etc. This book isn't trying to gloss over those realities.

But for those who are in a space of wondering why, even when they have their basic needs met, they still hold onto anxiety around money and finances, consider viewing it as a useful tool—helpful but not entirely necessary. We can buy groceries or grow food in a container garden. We can buy a fancy house or teach ourselves some DIY skills to make our existing space more to our liking. We can learn how to cook fancy dishes without having to go out to a restaurant. We can go onto free-cycle forums, barter, shop yard sales or online marketplaces, and exchange items we might not need or skills we might have for things or services we might require. We could become a live-in caregiver or companion in exchange for a roof over our head. The point is not to make this list exhaustive but to show that thinking outside the norm of having to have *money* to buy what we want and need is something we've been conditioned to accept but has not always been the way.

## SAVE IT AND SPEND IT WISELY

There is an old Depression era slogan that goes: "Use it up, wear it out, make it do, or do without" which is still helpful to keep in mind today as we search for ways to repurpose, reuse, or upcycle things we might have discarded in the past. The reality we currently live in is, even with such efforts, life often requires money and most of us for environmental and ethical reasons would prefer not to be wasteful.

For most of us, if we want extra for "fun" things, we need to save it. This is not easy at all when one is scraping by, and one of the most direct ways to save is to pay ourselves first. Whatever amount we can set aside whether small or large, will eventually add up if we set it aside each payday before any other spending. Having a goal or reward we are saving up for makes this task an investment versus simply a slush fund to dive into whenever the mood hits.

When we've saved enough for the thing? Look for a sale, find the best deal, and if there's money left, call it seed money for the next expenditure on the wish list.

Oftentimes, though, we come across something we want, an impulse-buy in the making. One of the rules I set for my kids when they were very young was (especially if it wasn't on sale or clearance) was to wait a week. If at the end of the week they still wanted to spend their money on the thing, we could go ahead. Oftentimes they would have gotten to the week's end and realized that there was something that suited their needs better or the thing they thought they wanted had lost its appeal. A cooling off or wait-and-see approach to temper impulse buys is very useful. Sometimes I take a picture with my phone of the item and tag, so I can look the item up online to price compare or even see if it truly fits my space, décor, or needs.

If the item is on sale or clearance or a find in a thrift store or any other this-is-your-only-chance situation, we would ask ourselves: I want it, but do I *need* it? Do I already have something that could fill this need? Could I find this same item for a better price or condition elsewhere?

Sometimes we just come across something fun or funky and we love it. If we are on the fence about whether we or the intended recipient would really want or have a place for it, take a photo and share the photo. It's likely all we wanted was to share the moment of discovering something fun with someone who can share that delight.

Another approach to curbing impulse buys is to have a "fun money" fund specifically for that piece of adorable décor, that gift for ourselves, or that special treat. This life is meant to be lived and enjoyed, so allowing ourselves to indulge in small moments of joy takes the pressure off the sense of deprivation that comes with feeling we have to save money only for important needs instead of occasional wants.

In summary: “wait and see”, shop with a known inventory of needs or shopping list, and find ways to re-use, re-purpose, or re-home items you have or others are done with.

## SPEND MONEY ON EXPERIENCES VS. THINGS

If I could tell my younger self anything about money and spending it would be this: invest in people, experiences, and original art.

Invest in the creative products of others. The books. The paintings. The glass blown sculptures. The pottery. Buy handmade jewelry straight from the artist. Attend small, local concerts and performance events. Surround yourself and infuse your world with the creations and experiences which speak to your soul and remind you every day of what the human imagination is capable of.

In that same vein, spend money investing in yourself: your skills, hobbies, interests, and experiences. Learn to cook or paint or weld or garden. Spend spare money on enhancing the things you already enjoy. This isn’t about hoarding a thousand action figures *unless* you use them in role-playing games or another interpersonal creative outlet. It’s not about accumulation; it’s about enhancing and enriching your world with memories and connection.

Most anyone who has traveled will tell you it’s the best money they have ever spent. Go ahead, ask them. If a destination vacation doesn’t fit your budget or lifestyle, consider going to a free concert, a museum that offers discounted admittance or free days, go on a nature hike, or a stroll through the streets of a picturesque city center. Whatever you choose to do, whether it’s zip-lining, a spa day, game board night with friends, or something in between, experiences with other people provide more long-lasting satisfaction than any *thing* we could acquire. Studies show that the act of planning an experience, having it, and looking back on it not only cements the memories for us, but also gives us three or more opportunities to be in the space of "enjoying" it.

I'm also going to push back on the idea that an unpleasant travel experience will ruin the whole positive aspects of it, because, as someone who has laid her cheek on the cool tile floor of our apart-hotel in Edinburgh when I came down with a nasty case of norovirus, I have a story to tell, and stories bring us together in shared human experience. The trained squirrel I tried to take a picture of on the bridge in Prague which was clearly a scam to get tourists to open their wallets? No worries. It's another story! (I didn't fall for it. I have the picture in my mind's eye.) For every missed train, heat wave or torrential downpour, closed for renovations sign on a landmark we'd hoped to visit, there were tiny parks nestled in the heart of the city, amazing local eateries that weren't on any tourist blog, the views of nature and buildings we'd only ever seen in books or online, the sense that we were standing on the land of our ancestors and seeing this place through their eyes not our own, and people eager to talk about what makes us all different and the same.

If I can urge you to do anything in this life, it's to move outside your comfort zone, push the boundaries of the everyday, and see some other part of this world which calls to you. It is never too soon or too late. You have this one life in this body, and it has never been easier to research your destination and make plans.

PART 7

# GRIEF

# Chapter 10

## GRIEF

My son was just six years old when he lost his first pet. Boo Bear was our tuxedo kitty. He was my "baby" before my first human baby. He was the cat who waited on the counter just inside the door for me to scoop into my arms the moment I got home each evening. He wanted to be held constantly: while I cooked, while we slept, and, after my son was born, even while I nursed.

### PLANTING LOVE

As my son grew, Bear adopted him as a brother, and the two became inseparable.

But then Bear took a turn, and the morning my husband had to leave to help his mother move apartments, I was left at home with a 6-year-old, a 2-year-old and a dying cat.

I knew it was too late as I carried Bear to the car, his fragile body growing oddly heavy in my arms as the life that had lifted him up to my shoulders countless times left him. We drove to the vet anyway. They confirmed what I already knew.

At home, I tried to stay strong for my son, as he helped me choose the right spot to bury his beloved friend, a shaded area by the back stone wall under the trees but close enough to visit. I will never forget how my heart broke as I carried the shovel across the back yard, my son sobbing at my heels, his dead cat wrapped in a towel held tightly in his small arms.

My own tears blurred my sight as I made the hole deep and wide enough. Nothing prepares you for parenting a broken-hearted child. The reality of hitting roots, knowing I was the only one home to cut through them made me resentful that there was no one to call to hug me, hold me.

We lay the towel, Bear, and a few cat toys in the hole, and I struggled with how to make sense of it all for myself much less the grieving child at my side.

"We're planting love today," I whispered to my son, encouraging him to sift some of the loose soil over the grave. "I know it hurts, but the love you feel for Bear in here…" I put my palm to his tiny chest. "It doesn't die with him. When we bury someone we love, it's like planting a seed. The love takes time to rest, and sometimes it seems so dark—that's grief. But then, when the time is right, sometime in the future we can't yet predict, it will grow again. When love grows again, you'll remember Bear and the love you had for him and that new love? It will be even bigger than you remembered. I promise you."

Later that summer we learned of a farm kitty who'd had kittens. It was time for love to bloom again.

It's incredibly hard to process grief as a child. I remember being an inconsolable kindergartener after my kitten, Zipper, ran away when the neighbors came to take care of her while we were out of town. I remember crying on the bus on the way to middle school the day after our young cairn terrier had bolted out the door into traffic.

It didn't get easier to come home from college for a weekend to learn our husky was rapidly failing. I found him lying on the cool basement floor, my father's face telling me all I needed to know. The next morning, my father, tears streaming down his face, carried our dog's lifeless body up the long stairs to bury him in the woods behind the back yard.

I held Zipper (II) in my arms as she took her last breaths after being hit by a car, and stroked the fur of countless other animals as the vet stared across at me before I gave one final nod of consent.

Death is an inevitable part of living, and grief is the price we pay for loving.

For the countless times I've had to face the last moments of a pet's life, not once have I allowed the inevitable heartbreak to get in the way of the joy of choosing to bring an animal into our home. Love never dies. It simply lays dormant in our hearts until the time is right for it to bloom again.

## EASY GRIEF

I lost my father after an extended illness when I was thirty-one years-old. He was diagnosed with ALS and died thirteen months later. Losing someone to a terminal disease is one of the hardest forms of grief, because it is a fatal train we see coming—the one that will eventually hit us—yet we are powerless to move out of the way. Anticipatory grief means we imagine what the end will look like, how it will come to pass, in a thousand different gut-wrenching ways. And, to be honest, when I finally got the news that my father had passed, it was almost a relief, because my mind could stop forming scenarios. I finally knew that *this* was what his death would look like. I also knew I could finally get on with the rest of the grieving process.

My mother passed many years later. While she had a degenerative auto-immune disease, it wasn't in itself terminal. We all knew she likely wouldn't live into her nineties but we still had time to visit and play games and live life, to share our milestones with her. My mother was also a woman who lived in a space of gratitude, so even though she was slowly and inevitably losing her independence, she always expressed gratitude for the support she had. She made caring for her and caring about her easy and uncomplicated, and so when the end came, as much as it came as a surprise that 'today was the day we'd say goodbye', it was blessedly quick in the scheme of things. We were able to ensure she was in no pain, and her passing was peaceful.

As the days unfolded after her death, as sad as I was to have lost her, I told people I was okay, and I was and still am these several years later, because, "It's an uncomplicated grief." I had no messy feelings about my relationship with my mother whom I loved dearly but for whom I also knew death was a physical relief. She had lived long enough to see my children born and grow and graduate high school. She had lived long enough to see me published. Her affairs had been "in order" for some time, and there were no messy family dynamics that would make handling her estate difficult. So, grieving was straight-forward—easy. There was no bargaining to give me more time with her, as I'd been gifted years of treasured moments after her diagnosis. There was no anger that she'd been dealt a raw deal, because she lived her life to the fullest, loved, traveled, created things. There were no regrets about things unsaid, because I told her I loved her often and she returned the same.

As a result, I grieved her loss but quickly moved to acceptance.

Uncomplicated relationships full of love and open communication tend to allow for uncomplicated grieving. Yes, we might experience the stages of grief, but moving through the early stages toward acceptance tends to happen more quickly and the transition is less fraught. That's not true, unfortunately, for everyone.

## COMPLICATED GRIEF

It's a lie we often tell ourselves that our complicated relationships will be made easy once that person dies. No more angry words or cutting remarks. No more gaslighting, manipulation, or physical or emotional abuse. All of that ends when that person is gone and good riddance! Right?

The trouble is, messy relationships in life lead to complicated grief in death. And, no, it's usually not our twisted psyche mourning the person, per se. What we mourn and grieve for are the possibilities that end with that person. Gone, too, is any hope of that emotionally-distant parent telling us they love us just as we are. Gone is the hope of being told we are good enough or that they are proud of us. Gone is the possibility of that person who wronged us in life offering a genuine and heartfelt apology. Gone is the chance for them to make amends. If in life we held onto a faint hope of a possibility of something good coming from that complicated, messy relationship we held with someone, once they are gone, we grieve for the possibilities that are no longer possible. We no longer have the option to tell this person, perhaps, how much or in what manner they harmed us. We no longer have the opportunity to set a boundary and hold it strong as proof that we did what we could to protect ourselves against toxic behaviors.

When a person dies with whom we've had complicated feelings, it leaves us mired in unprocessed emotion: anger, regret, grief for what *could have been*, confusion about our worth or the part we played in the dysfunction of that relationship.

So how does one move through complicated grief?

You won't like this, but my experience is: slowly. Intentionally. While there is no longer an opportunity to address all the complex feelings in person and face-to-face, it can be helpful to speak them out loud to a close friend, therapist, trusted clergy person, or in writing in the form of a letter to the deceased. Avoid talking to other family members about the deceased especially if they have their own complex feelings. Even if you both understand the relationship "from the inside," talking about your trauma or complicated feelings may be mutually triggering, so be mindful of that.

## UNDERSTANDING GRIEF

It can be helpful to understand a few things about grief regardless of whether the relationship with the deceased was complex or uncomplicated:

**Grief has no timeline.** It may take days, weeks, months, or years to feel "normal" again, but grief is a feeling that can spring up when our memory is triggered, so don't be surprised if you feel you are "okay" and then out of nowhere find yourself near tears. Milestone events, birthdays, even holidays can bring us back into our feels in the blink of an eye. It's normal, and, eventually, will grow less pronounced.

**We don't "get over" death so much as learn to live with it.** When I mention "normal" above I don't mean to imply that anyone who has lost a loved one gets over missing them or reaches a point of forgetting about their loss. Normal means that we will come to a day where we don't think about the loss. It will become like any other major event in our life, like a birth or a graduation, that while impactful isn't a memory that has to hijack our emotions. Normal means that we are able to go on with living without feelings of sadness or guilt that we are here on this mortal plane and they are not.

**Grief remains the same size. Life gets bigger around it.** There is a famous analogy shared by Lauren Herschel for the grieving process called "the ball in the box" which explains that when we first experience a loss, grief is a big, ball bouncing around a box where we feel pain each time the ball happens to hit the pain button. At first, the box is small, and the pain button is frequently triggered. Over time, however, as our life continues, the box grows bigger, so while the ball is the same size and still occasionally touches the pain button, it does so less frequently and with less intensity.

**Grief can be additive.** I remember the first funeral I went to after the passing of my father. It was at least a year or more later, and the deceased was an acquaintance but not someone in my daily life. But, as I sat in that church and listened to the eulogy, I felt a wave of grief so profound I struggled to contain my sobs. I realized, then, that my body was remembering the grief of losing my own father, and I was empathizing with the family who'd lost their grandfather, father, and husband. Just as attending a wedding can remind you of the joy of your own marriage or the beauty of love, I realized that grief can also be a feeling we remember on a physiological level. I suppose I say this to warn you that being human is messy and that the funeral of someone we only briefly knew or standing in the greeting card aisle around the holidays can be major ball-in-a-box moments.

**Grief can become a pattern if we let it. Be careful of making "grieving" your identity.** It's perfectly normal to remember the date a loved one passed, to gather pictures of that loved one in a special place in our home, or to wear their favorite sweater as a remembrance. No one wants to "forget" their loved one, and many feel it is a way of honoring those who have passed to keep their memory alive. But at what point do these normal stages of the grieving process and personal memorials to those we've loved become a hurdle for the grief-stricken?

I have known siblings who lost their mother, and for years after would share memes on social media about how hard it is to lose one's mother, how eternally they will grieve for their beloved mother, etc. The other siblings chime in with their own grief. Viewing it from the outside it sometimes feels as if they are in an echo chamber of grief, almost as if they are in competition for who is more saddened by the loss. Seldom if ever do I recall reading anecdotes of loving their mother in her life—shared memories—it is always a message of grief and loss, and if it doesn't begin there it ends on a mournful note. Because these siblings are all in the space of feeling and sharing their grief this way, they don't appear to be moving forward through the grieving process. They appear stuck.

As I mentioned before, my father died when I was thirty-one. It was late April. I remember the year because I happened to be seven months pregnant with my first-born. I remember the month because it was also my father's birth month, and we'd just celebrated his birthday not long before. I never remember the day. I would have to look up his obituary or death certificate to remember the day he died, but why would I? I want to remember my father not at his end, where his body had wholly given out on him, but in his most vibrant, loving, life-filled moments. I want to remember his face as his eyes glistened with love and connection right before he walked me down the aisle. I want to remember holding his hand long after it was probably socially-acceptable to do so, because I was his youngest and he was my dad. I want to remember him ditching his truck on the side of the road and scrambling out, leaving me inside the cab, because he was deathly afraid of stinging insects and a bee had flown in the window. I want to remember the night he heard me coughing as a college student and quietly came and knocked on my bedroom door to offer cough syrup. I want to remember him patiently showing me how to wire an outlet, swing a hammer, split wood, or make his spicy jambalaya. The date of his last breath is insignificant when I have millions of breaths and thousands of days to look back upon and relive in my memories.

Be careful, then, when grieving, to allow yourself to feel your sadness but not to lose yourself in it. Beware of making grief your identity or a competition. No one wins that game.

**It's okay to laugh while grieving. Laughter is a coping mechanism.** Have you ever laughed at a funeral? While telling a story about the deceased? If we fear we are sliding into the doldrums of grief, laughter can be hugely helpful in lifting us out again. It breaks grief apart so we can move through it more easily. Laughter helps grief feel less heavy on our hearts.

**You will remember other times. I promise.** It can be hard if someone's passing is particularly difficult or traumatic to feel safe in letting go of those final, vivid memories. Our minds replay traumatic scenes to the point where we want to block all memories of that person to protect ourselves, but in doing so we fear that we will "forget" the sound of our loved one's voice, or the scent of their cologne. I am here to tell you that our memories are wonderful things. We can let go of the difficult scenes. In time the sound of their laughter may grow faint, but then we will realize that our nephew laughs just that way. Or as the more traumatic memories fade, it leaves space for the quieter, calmer memories to bubble to the surface. Perhaps a loved one always brought a particular dish to family gatherings, or there was a time they stumbled into the lake in their Sunday best trying to take a picture. Random memories which bring us joy will pop into our mind when we least expect them. I invite you to notice them, remember your loved one in that moment in time in their life. Thank them for sharing this life with you, and place that treasured memory back in its special box. Set it on your memory shelf to enjoy another time.

Likewise, if the relationship was complicated and we have memories from earlier times that rise up which are hard for us to revisit, acknowledge whatever feelings those memories bring, take a breath, and let those hard feelings and memories rise up like balloons in the sky. They can exist somewhere *out there* wherever the wind might take them, but we don't have to make space in our lives or on our treasured memory shelves for those particular remembrances.

## IT ISN'T JUST ABOUT PEOPLE

We as a society have a lot of difficulty acknowledging and making space for messy human feelings. This is especially true of feelings we can't control or may not personally understand. Grief is one of those messy feelings that we don't like to talk about, because what if it's not easy grief but complicated grief? Will it hurt the person if we invite them to talk about it? Are we encouraging a pattern of grief if we acknowledge their sadness even though it's been months since the death? What do we say when someone is grieving? How do we phrase our support so it isn't dismissive?

Corporations try to manage grief by allotting a few days for the logistics of death. We are allowed a few days for immediate family.

One or two to attend a funeral of a "lesser" relative. It all feels ridiculous when we think about how family dynamics can make a grandmother a mother figure or an uncle like a father or brother. What we all neglect to acknowledge is that grief isn't an event, it's a feeling, and it can attach itself to loss of any kind.

We grieve lost pets, the loss of a marriage, the loss of a pregnancy. We can grieve lost opportunities, communities, or futures we'd imagined. Even "good" things can trigger grief. Retirement. Moving. Graduation or going off to college. We grieve the loss of a predictable past or structures that had given light or meaning or purpose to our days. We grieve our childhood innocence.

As I write this, I think of the number of people I know in my life *right now* who are experiencing sadness, and it reminds me that everyone you meet is struggling with something, relieved about something, looking forward to something, stressed about something.

Perhaps we have to accept that grief is as much a part of the human experience as breathing, and hold compassion and understanding for others and stop trying to pretend that three days is enough time to mourn a child.

As natural and universal as grief is, we must learn to recognize when someone needs help moving through their grief. (Notice I didn't say getting over it.) If we or a loved one are stuck in the grieving process unable to see how to move forward, it's time to call in assistance, whether that's calling a friend to ask them to come sit with us, reaching out to a trusted member of clergy or professional therapist or grief support group, the way to move through times of intense grief is to reach out to others.

It's okay to feel sad. It's normal to miss people and animals that were once central figures in our daily lives. It's normal to feel unmoored when the death of a prominent figure has us questioning how our lives and greater society will be impacted by this change.

Are we being called to step up for a leadership role in our family, community group, or friendship circle? Are we grieving our innocence or our relative carefree existence?

The thing I've learned about grief is that it has shown me some very dark and painful places, but in time, when I've reached high points and moments of joy? The distance from my previous grief magnifies the heights of that later joy. I lean into that joy with all I've got and dig in with both hands and my teeth. That laughter you hear? That is *belly* laughter. I make sure I am wholly present for any joy emotionally, physically, and spiritually, because—like grief—it, too, is temporary.

When grief hits us, it is okay to acknowledge the loss, to recognize that our feelings are valid and normal. But then? Open yourself in all your vulnerability to the possibility of joy. Allow yourself to swing high, to push out the walls of that box you exist in so that when grief finally touches the pain button again, it's cushioned by your laughter and intentional joy. Gratitude slows the speed of your grief as it bounces within you, and laughter cushions the impact. Neither takes away or diminishes your grief or dishonors a departed loved one. Joy allows us to live with our grief. It expands the box we live in. That is all.

## GRIEF AND SELF CARE: NAVIGATING HOLIDAYS

I want to speak a moment about the side of the holiday season that doesn't get as much attention but is a vital part of both self-care and compassion. While some of us look forward to holidays and family gatherings, others dread them.

For those for whom it is the first holiday without a loved one, I see you. I have walked the bittersweet tightrope of grieving during a season of joy, and it can feel both lonely and disorienting. My message to you is to let yourself remember the love! Let it flow when it asks to, share it with those who understand your heart's tenderness, and be as gentle with yourself as a quiet new-fallen snow. Your life has changed, and you're allowed to feel sorrow. You are, also, allowed to feel joy! And I would wager, your loved one loved to see you smile. It's okay to be in your messy feels. The human experience *is* messy... and beautiful. If you are able, sit in gratitude that you experienced the joy of sharing some of life's journey with someone so special. And stock up on tissues, the lotion kind. ((HUGS)) to you.

Maybe, though, your holidays will be difficult not because of those who are missing but because of the people still in them. If you struggle because of others' expectations of you (expectations=premeditated resentment, let that sink in for a moment), hear this: boundaries are self-care. Let's repeat for those in the back: boundaries are self-care.

Those who love you will respect them even if they don't fully understand the reasons for them yet. And if you are made to feel guilty for setting boundaries, if those without our best interests at heart claim our boundaries are hurting them, know that this is a false framing.

---

*Boundaries are not weapons but the armor and shields we use to protect us from harm.*

---

A boundary is a healthy response to another's misbehavior. If they are free to continue to act out, we are free to enrobe ourselves in the pink bubble of peace.

This was a long-winded way of saying: move through this time with compassion and self-care. And when you are fortunate enough to be in the presence of those who bring you peace, safety, and love

I wish for you to throw open your doors and greet them with open hearts and gratitude. And cookies. Cookies for everyone!

## HONORING THE DEAD: CELEBRATIONS, PROMISES, & THINGS

Death is a weird transition. On the one hand, it seems that that person might somehow come back to judge how we've grieved, how much we've grieved, whether we've grieved in acceptable ways, and whether we've upheld our promises and honored their dying wishes. On the other hand, death is final in that we are the only ones left on this mortal plane, so what are we doing all this for? Us and those around us.

I want to gently nudge those of us who are holding on to an ugly thing that was never wanted but was gifted by a deceased loved one: it is okay to hold the love and rehome the object. It is okay to acknowledge that a promise made to someone who passed was a strong suggestion and not an immortally-binding contract. Your loved one will know the depths of your love regardless of whether you make a public display, an elaborate memorial, or post on social media every anniversary of their passing. It is okay and right to move on with the life you still have if that feels right.

Celebrate the lives of those who passed before us. Honor their memories when they are naturally remembered, and let go of all other expectations which weigh on the heart.

## EXPRESSING SYMPATHY AND HOW TO EASE GRIEF FOR OTHERS

Years ago, I stopped at our local vet's office to pick something up when a woman stepped from the door to my left. I knew the room well. I'd been there myself. It was the room the vet used to euthanize pets, because there was a back door through which staff could take the body to your vehicle for home burial.

The woman stood in the small lobby, arms empty, and her face said it all. I could see her world was shattered. I didn't have to ask what was wrong.

I'm typically more reserved as a rule, being a New Englander, but as I wordlessly met her eyes, I stepped forward, and opened my arms in invitation.

She stepped into my arms, and I hugged this stranger, saying nothing, just being present with her and supporting her in her grief. We both cried, her for her beloved pet, and me because to be truly present with someone is to feel what they feel.

When she could compose herself, she inhaled a deep breath and let go, nodding a small thanks.

We never spoke.

In 2013, psychologist Susan Silk and her husband Barry Goldman developed a paradigm for how to compassionately provide comfort to those in crisis or grief. Called "Ring Theory" or "Circle of Support", simply described, the model says that whomever is in crisis sits in the center of a number of social circles. They are, essentially, the main character. Those closest to that person, often their nuclear family, are in the next circle. Then extended family or close friends. Then less-close friends. Maybe after that is coworkers and acquaintances. The model is simple: complaints about the crisis or pain point and its impact can only move from inner circles toward outer circles. Comfort and support? That moves from outer circles to inner circles.

In practice, this illustrates what most of us intuitively know: it's unfair to tell a loved one suffering from cancer how hard their illness is on *us,* but it's okay to tell our close friend how exhausted we are from worry and caregiving. The idea is we never burden the person closest to or experiencing the crisis with our complaints; those must be directed outward to those less involved and less impacted.

You should know that this model has its critics, and it certainly isn't intended to be the be-all-end-all in navigating interpersonal relations. What it is, is a guideline, and if you consciously ignore it, do so with intent and good reason.

When I offered a hug to that woman grieving that day, I was outside the impact of her loss and so it was my role to offer comfort and not, heaven forbid, complain about the vet running overtime or the bad weather or anything else I might have been feeling. Even if I were there to make an appointment for *my* dying pet, that moment? That was not for me. That was for *her*.

But now that we've established the direction comfort should flow, the next hurdle is knowing *how* to help.

We've all heard the remonstration to not tell a grieving person "I know how you feel." We also know we should avoid dismissive platitudes like "they are in a better place", "at least you have other children", "you'll find another job", "you are better off without that deadbeat", and other phrases which serve more to make the sympathizer feel better than they do to alleviate the despair of the grieving. So, what, *exactly* are we supposed to *say* when someone loses a loved one, gets a scary medical diagnosis, loses their job, or goes through a divorce?

I would suggest that instead of jumping in with something clichéd or pithy, we pause, and sit a moment with that person. Be in a space of likely discomfort. Express how sorry we are they are going through this rough period. Then, ask: Is there anything specific you need help with?

Maybe their response is that they are too tired or they haven't eaten and can't think of what they need help with. Then we know that they need help figuring out the next step. From there we can suggest they go lie down while we tidy up and make them something to eat. Or maybe they don't even have groceries. We can ask them their favorite comfort foods and go buy a bag or two of easily-prepared meals for them. Or we can take the time to put together a simple meal to share with them so they remember that they are still capable of these self-sustaining tasks and are worthy of our company even when they are feeling at their lowest. Perhaps they are worried about finances or how they will navigate legal issues. We might offer to go with them to consult a lawyer or financial planner.

Perhaps, though, they simply need to talk about what they are going through—to process it aloud to someone who won't judge them or try to leap-frog to a happier timeline.

Not long ago a dear friend was navigating a particularly difficult time. She'd lost a beloved pet, a parent was walking the path of advancing memory loss, and her job and the world were proving to be sources of added stress and not comfort. She was a working mom with a full-time job and aging parents and while the outside world expected her to soldier on, she was crumbling inside.

I asked her one day if she had time to sit with me. She nodded. We found a quiet space and sat.

I allowed myself to be in her space, to feel the heaviness of the burden she was carrying as it sat with us. I told her I could tell she was struggling and that I was here for her. I wanted her to know I had been praying for her, and I was sorry she was having such an obviously difficult time.

I gave her the space to speak what was so heavily on her heart, not trying to solve it but to bear witness to her pain—to acknowledge and validate that what she was experiencing was hard.

We both shed tears. We hugged. And as we hugged, I said to her: "Please. Allow me to share your grief. I promise you I'm strong enough to handle it."

She nodded again, and breathing a deep sigh of relief, shared more of her sadness at time marching on, worrying that the career she'd dedicated her life to wasn't having the impact she'd hoped for, and all the other messy fears and feelings we too often don't feel we're allow to speak aloud. We sat there for a long while as she shared all that she'd been burdened with and how sad it was making her.

I could change none of it. I was helpless to bring her dog back, reverse the disease taking her beloved father, overpower the societal realities that weighed so heavy on her heart. I made a couple suggestions about how to set boundaries which was probably more for me to feel I was doing something useful, and then I thanked her for sharing with me.

Sometimes when we are struggling it isolates us to the point we feel we are struggling alone. But that doesn't have to be. Often just knowing someone is there to sit with us in our grief is enough to lighten the load. So, if you are ever struggling with what to say or do to comfort someone who grieves? Be with them. Just *be* with them. Treat them as you would someone who broke a bone and is laid up and feeling behind. Assist with practical matters as appropriate and then reassure them that you are there for them. And mean it.

Because in the end, if everything else in this material world is lost to us, that which would most bring us comfort is the presence of another loving, comforting, understanding soul.

PART 8

# ADVERSITY & RESILIENCE

# Chapter 11

## ILLNESS, INJURY, & ADVERSITY

### WHAT HEALTH CHALLENGES CAN TEACH US

Several years ago, one of my kids faced a scary medical diagnosis which required a biopsy, multiple interventions, and, ultimately, major knee surgery. They went from being a happy-go-lucky teen to crutches and a surgery date within a matter of days and all within a month of graduation.

We had to consider the AP exam schedule while threading the needle of all the special end-of-high-school events they wanted to attend as well as jump through hoops of getting COVID vaccines—and to say it was *a lot* is to understate things.

Unfortunately, it wasn't a situation that resolved quickly, and we were still scheduling medical care and recovery time throughout their freshman year of college. Amidst this, they decided to transfer schools. Then their dad fell ill, and their grandmother passed away, all before they were to be told, a year from when it all began, that the more invasive surgery they'd hoped to avoid would be needed after all.

Yes, it was a hard year. I won't tell you there weren't tears during this time, but as we navigated those difficult months, it reminded me of what I'd said at the very beginning of the pandemic lockdowns: "We're going through some really difficult times and none of us has a crystal ball about how it's going to turn out. But at the end of this—and it will eventually be behind us—do you want to have wrung your hands and fretted about your circumstances, or do you want to have made the best of things and made a plan for where you want to be and what you want to have accomplished when all this is behind you?"

---

*"When all this is over and in the rearview mirror, what will you wish you had done? What do you want to have accomplished? Who do you want to have been? Focus on that now. We don't know how long this will last or how long we have. Make your plans."*

---

We all, *all of us,* experience challenging times. Sometimes a lot of challenges all at once, sometimes collectively in our community, nation, or world. We can either allow those challenges to sideline us and derail us from our paths, or we can decorate our crutches with flowers and wear the masks and attend our outdoor proms, allowing ourselves to adapt to the realities of the moment without sacrificing our goals for the long-term.

Like the age-old meme for those of a certain age: *Pivot!*

## BEING AT PEACE WITH LOSS OF CONTROL

The Serenity Prayer spoken so often by those facing addiction is a familiar verse for many of us:

---

*"God, grant me the serenity to accept the things I cannot change, the courage to change the things I can, and the wisdom to know the difference."*

---

Embedded in this verse is the notion that some things, probably a lot of things, are outside of our immediate control. What happens to us, our bodies, our loved ones, is often a matter of chance, genes, circumstances, or past decisions, and nothing in any given moment will change that.

Recognizing that the only thing that *is* ever under our control is our response to any current moment, can provide a sense of peace. We can free ourselves from self-flagellation for actions taken in the past, as they are done. We cannot undo them. Actions and behaviors of others are also outside of our control, so we can let go of those, too. Letting go of anger at or disappointment in our prior actions or decisions, or the actions or decisions of others, frees us to be present in this moment for ourselves. Here we are. *Right here.* We are experiencing something, whether we perceive it as good, bad, or neutral. What do we choose as our next action? What is the next best step? Our response to any given moment is always, *always* a choice.

In Part 9 I talk more about decision-making strategies for when we feel stuck or uncertain, but for this moment, be at peace. Let go of any illusion of control you thought you had over the outer world when things were going well, because that, too, was an illusion. Should you find yourself in a dark place, look for the light, look for the helpers, look for the encouragement of your own track record of surviving life thus far, and choose your response.

Make your plans.

# Chapter 12

## RESILIENCE

### WHEN BAD THINGS HAPPEN TO GOOD PEOPLE

Over the course of one eventful year, my husband was hospitalized multiple times. He suffered sepsis, encephalopathy, and organ damage. More than once, we'd been asked if we had advance directives and urged to prepare for the worst. He was placed on disability from a job that had defined his personal identity for decades. Our youngest had, after a year of painful and ultimately unsuccessful interventions, undergone bone graft surgery in their femur. In the midst of all that, my mother suddenly passed away. In short, our lives were in upheaval.

Not long after my husband was released from a ten-day hospital admission for a massive infection the doctors struggled to bring under control, we ran into one of his work colleagues.

We assured her we were doing as best as could be expected given all that had happened and that he felt lucky to be alive.

What she said was something we'd heard before, and it gave me pause. She said, "I just feel so badly for you. You're such good people and to have all this happen…"

She trailed off, trying to make sense of hard things happening to otherwise "good" people however that's defined. It didn't sit well with me, though, this notion that some people deserved hardships like sudden illness or accidents or loss and other people should be immune to life's challenges.

"Why *not* us?" I asked. "Who else or what other family would I wish this on? As hard as it's been, I feel like if this should happen to anyone, let it be us.

"We have the means and insurance to care for him, access to a well-regarded medical facility, and the support of family and friends who have been there as shoulders to cry on or to deliver meals when we couldn't identify what do to next. No. It's okay that this should happen to us. We're going to be okay, because as hard as it's been, we're not alone. We don't have to go through it alone."

I'll be one hundred percent real with you, it wasn't easy to get to the place of pushing back on the narrative that the overwhelming and scary things happening in our lives were undeserved because we were "good." But to accept that we don't deserve such experiences implies that someone else *does*. There is no part of my brain that can wrap itself around some truly horrific experiences out there I've read about nor can I wrap my brain around having any of that awfulness be something *deserved* by the least and most innocent amongst us. Do children deserve cancer? Do victims deserve shocking abuse? Does anyone deserve poverty, war, or disease? Does a parent deserve to lose a child? Of course not.

Taken to the extreme, it's clear that no one deserves difficult times or experiences, these things simply *are*. Awful things happen, seemingly at random, but we can decide for ourselves whether we believe that and to what extent. All I know is that these things did happen to us. We didn't foresee them, and it's hard to imagine at what point we made a decision to consciously move toward them happening.

So, once they happened, what then? If we all at some point will come across adverse circumstances, how do we cope?

---

*Lean in.*
*Connection is the key to coping with hardship.*

---

It's human nature to pull away and retreat to our protected corners when things go haywire, but as our lives were thrown into turmoil, I realized that that's the opposite of what we should be doing. We needed to think of ourselves as like stones in an arch. If any one of us retreated, pulled away, everything would crumble. But—if we leaned in—if we turned toward one another and remained open to one another, we had a better shot at withstanding the challenges we faced.

*Remains of stone chimney, Dunnottar Castle, Scotland*

You might be saying, that's all well and good, but what if we're not facing a life-altering situation so much as difficulty, annoyance, or injustice?

---

*Be the water. Flow over, under, and around your obstacles. Wear obstacles away with steady, dogged persistence toward your goal.*

---

This is the advice I gave my headstrong kids throughout the years, particularly as they railed against perceived injustices. It's a reminder that sometimes we are not in a position or don't have the strength to push aside obstacles in our path. In those cases, we can learn from water. Water always finds a way. It may take time, but having an end-goal and working steadily toward it, will almost always get us there.

## WORRY NOT

I've said it to my family many times:

---

*Worry is just forcing you to live through a thousand awful possibilities which may never come to be.*

---

Do you listen to yourself when you speak? Do you hear the words you repeat to yourself? Tune in for a moment. Any time we tell ourselves something "always" or "never" happens, we should take note. That's usually pointing toward an internal belief. If that belief makes us feel victimized or helpless in any way, that is a *limiting belief.* These beliefs of "the way the world is" are often inherited, absorbed during our formative years, or a result of trauma of some sort.

Limiting beliefs are areas for evaluation and growth. If we place ourselves in a space of believing something "always" or "never" happens, we have made ourselves believe we don't have (or never will have) the power to change that thing. If worry is a mindset of living a thousand worst-case scenarios for the future, then limiting beliefs are a mindset which rob us of agency in the present moment.

Hope is the remedy for limiting beliefs, because it exists in the space of asking ourselves: "What if?"

---

*Hope helps us think in possibilities. Hope allows us to imagine the many pathways there are to joy.*

---

What if how things have been for us in the past doesn't dictate how they will be in the future? What if the resources we had when we were younger, in a different place, with different people, have changed for the better?

When we challenge these limiting beliefs, it allows us to move away from anxious or fatalistic mindsets.

## MOVING FROM "NOW WHAT?!?" TO "WHAT IF?"

Resilience isn't a once and done thing, and being resilient often doesn't feel particularly good when we are in the in-between state of difficult change. How do we even know if we are resilient and what does it even mean? I think of resilience as the ability to move from paralysis to hope again. It is the difference between waiting for outside help versus problem solving even when overwhelmed by the messiness of life. It's the willingness, when a helping hand is offered, to put in the effort to grab onto it even when we are down in the muck.

The human brain is "plastic" as they say. Like a ski slope or sledding hill, the more we take a specific path, the more our brain will follow that path in the future. What that means is that it's super important not to get too stuck or comfy wallowing in the space we don't want to be, but to—as quickly as we're able—get ready to push off. Sometimes that takes outside help, a little push if you will, but then taking that path toward solution or resolution or better times? That becomes easier the more we practice. The path we choose can lead us right back to a place of being stuck… or off and away toward a place of hope and happiness.

Be wary of conflating being victimized with victimhood. One is something that happened *to* us; the other is a mindset we adopt. One is an experience (albeit a negative one) and the other is an identity. It's understandable to be upset at being victimized, but we shouldn't let those who have harmed us determine our identity, too. We've earned the title of "survivor"!

## SURVIVING VS. THRIVING

I am an avid DIY-er. My husband and I have drawn up plans, bought supplies, hired professionals when needed, and embarked on numerous home improvement projects and additions over the years. I successfully homeschooled my children, one through junior high. (I say successfully, because both have now completed advanced or post-secondary degrees at this point.) After years of an ever-fickle and changing market for fiction, I embarked on teaching myself how to self-publish my own novels and have successfully done so, having earned enough from my efforts to support my daughter's years of equestrian lessons and competitions.

This is all to say that I consider myself someone who has repeatedly set goals, worked toward them, and attained if not the goals I began with, enough of them to feel satisfied with my efforts.

But then my goal-oriented, positive-thinking, "be the water" advice-giving self hit a wall. I found myself experiencing a presidential administration that felt chaotic and even hostile, my mother-in-law reached the end of a toxic and unhappy life, my own mother's health declined in lock-step, the pandemic hit and closed down all the usual ways I felt connected with others, then my kid received a scary medical diagnosis, within months I lost my mother, my husband had his own health crisis, and if all of this wasn't enough, I was called in for a colonoscopy after some results from a preliminary screening came back with concerns. (All is well, but do go for your healthcare screenings!)

You will probably laugh when I only now, three years later, realize that the reason I stopped feeling capable of creative thought and struggled to finish a manuscript during that time is because, newsflash, I was expending all my energy on surviving.

I was surviving.

---

*When going through hell, keep going.*
~ Winston Churchill

---

Sometimes, surviving is all we are capable of.

And if you are only surviving in this very moment? *Good.* Keep doing that. Stay the course. Persist. This human existence is hard and wonderful and all things in between, and we endure the hard times so that we can get to see and feel those highs. We have to give ourselves the grace to exist in the in-between space of traveling from thriving to surviving and back again. No, we won't always be on that upswing, and it's often not a result of any choice we made that we find ourselves sliding down that slippery slope to survival.

It's true. We won't always thrive, but that is the goal, and it's attainable! Thriving involves learning sometimes tough life lessons about our own resiliency, our inner and community resources, our own role in our current circumstances, and even our own self-limiting beliefs and self-sabotaging behaviors. Unraveling *all that*—undoing what might need reworking or rebuilding—sometimes requires us to tear it all down and start building a new foundation for ourselves with the hard-earned knowledge we've gained from past mistakes.

But it's never too late to tear down or start anew. It's never too late.

I remember as a young teen learning that Edgar Allen Poe had written *The Raven* when he was but 19 years old. Just nineteen! I thought to myself, that surely, if he could do that at such a young age, I was capable of the same. But then my nineteenth birthday came and went without an internationally-lauded poem to my credit, and I thought, "Hmm. Fine. I will write a novel by the time I'm thirty!" I started it, then I got a job, got married, bought a fixer-upper house, proceeded to renovate it, added on a large addition, said goodbye to my father, had a baby, lost my job, found another, had a miscarriage, got critically ill, and *then* finished my first novel.

I wrote several more books before seeking publication, got very close. Wrote another book. The market experienced wild turmoil. I had another child. I told myself I'd be published by forty.

Well into my forties, I took my journey into my own hands. I was done waiting on others to make my dreams come true and took the steps to bring my first manuscript to market. In doing so, I joined a long, long list of those who have found that age is a number but is otherwise meaningless. Writing a poem, whether at 19 or 87, doesn't affect the merits of the work. So, pursue your passions, hobbies, goals, wherever and whenever in life it works for you, and know that that is the right time to pursue it.

## WHEN WE ARE AFRAID TO TRUST GOOD NEWS

One of the major obstacles I've noticed to feeling free to believe in something 'better'—to hope—is feeling able to trust after trauma or heartache. Let me explain. For those who have experienced trauma, trusting the calm that comes with true joy can be difficult. Survival is what we've learned, and so we look for reasons to pull out our trusty survival skills. We might catastrophize or shy away from allowing ourselves to revel in good experiences or feelings, because we're waiting for the other shoe to drop and the chance to say "I knew it would happen" as we strap on our trusty survival toolbelt.

Perhaps we've had our heart broken, and so the relative peace and lack of drama experienced with a new friend or partner feels suspicious to us instead of comforting. We might find ourselves distrustful of the ease with which things are progressing without the excitement and drama of past, albeit unhealthy, relationships.

I have known people who, early in life, lost a beloved pet and thereafter vowed they would never have another pet, because that loss was so painful. They know they survived that first loss, but they don't trust themselves to be able to withstand another.

I understand all these reactions and there are times I've felt them. These are human responses to feeling pain. We want to minimize pain, so we dull our reactions and limit our exposure to experiences that have, in the past, hurt us. But in protecting ourselves from feeling potential pain, we also limit our potential joy.

As I think about the many animals I've welcomed into my life over the decades—and the number I've had to say goodbye to—I think about how much richer my existence has been for allowing that joy into it for however long it was meant to be. Those of us who are pet owners know this sad truth: we will likely outlive our pets, and yet how many of us joyfully adopt babies or seniors or those animals rescued from neglect? We do this *knowing* that however much grief our future self may experience, it will be more than offset by joy.

In human relationships it's only natural to feel that while we survived the last breakup we don't know if we would survive the next. So, we tread carefully. We modulate our elation with a new person. We temper our hopes.

We limit ourselves.

We limit ourselves to experiencing and feeling only as much happiness as we had before things went south in the past. We survived the fall from that height of happiness, so we don't allow ourselves to feel *more* joy just in case things fall apart again. Falling from any higher plane of elation might be too much to bear.

It has been said that pain is the universal human experience. We tell ourselves life is hard and often hurts, but we know how to survive!

We need to trust, though, that we can also thrive.

This is resilience. It is the ability to trust that good news is just that: good news! Resilience rejects the notion that we are meant to merely survive and insists that our universal birthright is to thrive.

Claim your birthright.

Don't limit your joy. Dive head-first into it! Swim in it. Shield your eyes as you look into its brightness and squint at the distant horizon of it. You will never regret the joy you've allowed yourself to experience. You will only regret not giving yourself a chance to feel it.

## OVERCOMING TRAUMA

As the Allen Saunders quote goes: "Life is what happens when you're busy making plans." It's a gentle reminder that while it's fine to plan for tomorrow, it's important to be present and appreciate today.

Let's be honest, though. Sometimes *this moment* of life is so brutal and difficult it makes it nigh on impossible to think about or even envision a tomorrow.

I am not a psychiatrist or trauma therapist. I absolutely encourage anyone dealing with any form of trauma or PTSD, addiction, or mental illness to consult a licensed professional. These people are trained to provide the type of compassionate and skilled care needed to help navigate difficult emotional waters.

But in the end, what they provide is oftentimes the most profound and necessary component of healing from trauma: having someone listen without judgment, provide validation and a safe space to express our feelings, and the permission to let go of the anger, resentment, pain, confusion, despair, or grief we no longer wish to hold.

---

*Healing from trauma often means allowing ourselves to feel our past pain in the presence of a compassionate witness.*

---

Reach out to your primary physician, your company's EAP office or flip to the Appendix of this book for a list of resources and contact information which I hope may prove useful as a first step in reaching out for further, skilled assistance.

The unfortunate reality is that too often the mental health support services many need are not available or affordable. In the absence of those professionals, a trusted person from our faith practice or a good friend or family member can provide compassionate witness in our healing journey.

PART 9

# DECISION MAKING

# Chapter 13

## DECISION MAKING FOR THE REAL WORLD

### HOW TO MAKE DECISIONS AND MOVE OUT OF PARALYSIS

Resilience is all well and good once we have a bit of momentum, but that doesn't help when we are stuck in the last bit of the fight, flight, or freeze response. If we are paralyzed from indecision there are methods of moving out of that stagnation. The Circles of Impact model is helpful in deciding when or how we take action.

### Circles of Impact

In the digital age, we are flooded with information and alarming news and often it becomes overwhelming. We want to do "something" but determining the next best step is difficult.

I like to use the "Circles of Impact" model of deciding on a course of action when a decision about how or whether I take action has me paralyzed.

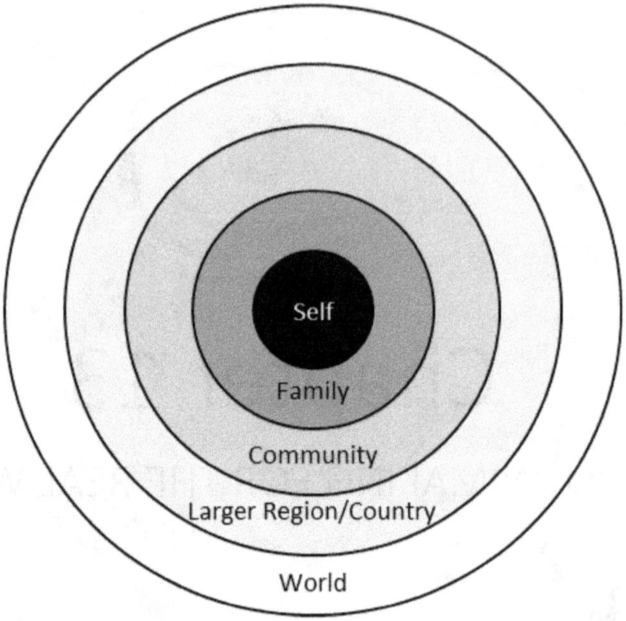


1) **Who is impacted?**
   The urgency with which—or whether—I take action depends on how close to the center of the graphic the perceived threat impacts. If it is me or my loved ones, I will want to take the first best step to mitigate risk or address the issue. Let's say I smell smoke and think the house is on fire. I will want to take immediate action.

2) **Do I have the tools, resources, or experience to help solve the issue?**
   I may feel perfectly capable of getting myself out of harm's way, but if it's a larger fire, or I have multiple people to evacuate, I will need help. Perhaps I don't feel I have the experience or resources to address the problem. Again, this is a prompt to ask for help.

3) **Do I need to ask for help?**
Sometimes, even if we think we *can* handle the problem ourselves, it's a good idea to notify others that we have a problem. Think of it as saying, "Hey, I smell smoke, I'm going in." This alerts those close to you that they should check in to see if the problem is resolved or we're in over our heads. If each of us does this, we can make others (those circles close to us) aware of threats which exist and are being addressed without causing undo alarm.

4) **Do I need to get out of the way?**
Maybe I want to resolve the problem, but I don't have the experience, personal resources, or know-how to help move toward a solution. In such times, making others aware of the threat but letting those better equipped address it is the better course of action.

5) **No action needed: Alert and Ready**
Maybe I thought I smelled smoke and it turned out to be my neighbor burning their brush pile. I see it's not in my yard, but I'm not sure they are being careful to keep it under control. In such cases, I will remain alert and ready to take action.

6) **Out of our control/Outermost circles**
Perhaps, though, the smoke I smell is from wildfires hundreds of miles away. In such cases, my responsive actions will be more removed and less immediately urgent. If I'm overwhelmed in taking care of other matters affecting my innermost circles of self and those closest to me, say we all have the flu, I can allow myself to feel less urgency about helping with wildfires far away. Perhaps I make a plan to give to wildlife relief charities when I'm feeling well

again, or I decide to help educate my community about how to mitigate the negative effects of climate change. Or, if I have the skills and resources, perhaps I decide to drive nearer to the wildfires to provide aid to the firefighting or relief efforts.

The point of the graphic is not to promote an "every person for themselves" mentality but to reassure those who don't have the bandwidth to take world-level action on every issue or crisis, that taking care of our innermost circles is, in fact, taking action. Our circles all overlap one another. As long as we remain connected with others, our overlapping circles of impact become Circles of Care. Always begin with taking care of yourself. Like the airline adage, "Use the oxygen mask on yourself first, then help those around you." We are of no use in helping others if depleted or struggling, so if we feel the need to help the world, we should make sure we are whole and well and cared for first.

What if, however, I am not directly affected and also cannot have any meaningful impact? If we simply take on someone else's worry as an empathetic person, you know what happens? Two people are now worried and anxious. My worry doesn't mitigate the concern of the first person and only serves to place me in a state of fight, flight or freeze. I can acknowledge that I have sympathy for them and their plight, and then, lovingly, let it go with a prayer that the solution can be found. I speak more on strategies to address anxiety in Chapter 23.

## OTHER DECISION-MAKING STRATEGIES

Sometimes our decisions aren't so much life or death as deciding which car to buy or whether to accept a job offer, and those decision strategies will look different than determining whether to act or not to a perceived "bad thing." That said, decision paralysis is real! So how do we figure out what's the right decision?

**Weighted-variables approach.**

When it's not as simple as a pro/con list, it can be helpful to give certain variables more weight in our decision-making process. Perhaps cost is a more pressing variable than the color of the car we want to buy, so we know that even if the car color is a pro and the cost is a con, we will give more weight getting a good deal than whether the car is our top color choice.

Things get stickier the less concrete each variable is, and that's where an iterative approach refines the weighted-variable approach.

**Iterative approach.**

Say we are deciding between two job offers with roughly the same benefits and salary. They may differ, then, in commuting distance, size of the company, office culture, advancement potential, and other hard-to-quantify variables. Maybe the company closer to home wants us to be on call, so the time spent on company time is roughly equivalent to the one further away. Here, it can be helpful to compare each variable to understand which hold more weight for us, especially useful for variables that are difficult to quantify.

In practice it would look like this: is office culture or flexible time off more important to me? Is flexible time off or advancement potential more important?" We continue comparing each variable to all others until we know which one carries the most weight for *us* (comes out on top the most often) and then apply that weight to our options.

**Intuitive decision making says go with your gut.**

Sometimes, though, we already know in our gut which way we are leaning even before we begin trying to justify our decision with numbers.

Years ago, I planned to meet my husband at a park-n-ride where I suggested he leave his car so that we could travel together to run errands in a city an hour south of us. The park-n-ride was closer to our destination but on his way home. He wanted to drive home and leave his car. I argued it saved time to meet at the park-n-ride, leave his car there, and continue in my vehicle. In the end, he acquiesced.

I wish he had held firm to his gut feeling. When we returned from our long evening of errands, exhausted two-year-old in the rear, we discovered someone had smashed his driver's side window and ransacked his car. Now, instead of saving time, I had to drive home and return with cleaning supplies so we could clear out the broken glass and get his car home and then follow up with the police department and insurance company.

Since that night, we've made an agreement that any time either of us has a gut feeling about something, we listen, no questions asked, no argument. We have agreed in advance that we will take the alternate route, pass up on the stop we'd planned, or otherwise trust that the intangible and unquantifiable *knowing* is just as important a factor in decision making as any quantified, rational argument.

I think of intuition as my subconscious mind being aware of subtle cues or factors my logical, conscious mind has not yet seen or processed. This "knowing" is equally if not more valid than our analytical mind, because those feelings or "knowings" are pure and not filtered through our limiting beliefs or ego.

In the end, listening to our gut for which choice to make is often not a terrible way to make a decision. Often, we tell ourselves we want a second opinion or more information because we don't trust that inner knowing. Or, we might feel judged for not having a readily defensible reason for wanting to lean a particular way.

When others are impacted by our decision, it's reasonable to seek their input. A community or consensus-based model makes sense for deciding on dinner for the family or which house we might like to move to. But if we're asking simply because we don't trust ourselves, there are some real flaws in this approach. Yes, a second opinion may well validate what our gut is already telling us. But, it's just as likely that that second person may have a perspective, bias, or preference that doesn't match ours, and their contrary opinion may well befuddle matters. If a decision will primarily affect me and not a larger social unit (say a family or business), outside input should be requested with caution and only if I either have no preference or truly can't discern my preference. Sometimes having someone state a preference is all it takes to reveal our own.

**Say no to buyer's remorse!**

Finally, avoid second-guessing decisions. Once made and decided, unless there is a fundamental change in some decision variable, do not look back. There will be no checking sales flyers for the item we just purchased and are currently enjoying. If we don't intend to take action on the knowledge that we could have gotten that appliance or car for less than we paid (as in, we don't plan to return the thing we bought) there's no point in browsing the ads or online sites for items we've already purchased. I say this with love: that ship has sailed. Move on!

## AVOID FEAR-BASED DECISIONS

It's all well and good to use a pro/con list for a new television or even whether or not to go forward with a house addition, but while it's helpful for less emotionally-fraught choices, how do we make decisions about relationships, whether to participant in our government, how much "emergency preparedness" is enough?

These decisions are often driven from a place of fear. Fear of being lonely or alone. Fear of "those other people" making decisions that negatively impact us. Fear of severe weather, civil unrest, or simply residual trauma from periods in our lives when we felt unprepared or wanting for food, shelter, or safety.

I'm not going to sit on my highly privileged horse and tell anyone what to do or when enough becomes too much. I will only make a few observations.

Be careful of making fear-based relationship decisions, as they almost always come from a place of being made to feel "less than." Assuming you are not approaching a potential relationship with a huge ego that demands a reward for being wonderful, if a potential friend or partner isn't making you feel better about yourself, that isn't the relationship for you. If you are ever told you can't do better? You most certainly can. Never settle. Never talk yourself into a relationship. Don't sell yourself short. You deserve the moon.

If you are thinking about becoming involved in community programs or government, please do so with hope, a vision for bettering the lives of others, and a sincere desire to be in community with and to listen to those you are serving. Those who run for office with a scarcity mindset or a desire to impose their preferences on others are headed for conflict.

When is 'enough' enough? I live in semi-rural New England. We routinely lose power for hours, sometimes several days, due to winter storms or summer winds. Knowing this, we take reasonable precautions, have invested in a back-up generator, and know where our flashlights are. Those in other areas have their storm shelters and hurricane supplies. My point is, for most of us, enough is defined as what we'd want to have on hand for several days knowing that in severe cases, our neighbors or larger communities would be there for us. We don't all have to own backhoes.

Some of us, though, hold anxiety or trauma that makes it more difficult to feel like we are prepared enough for the unknowingness of climate change and civil unrest. It is very hard to stop ourselves from hoarding that little bit more, or shedding that hyper-vigilance we feel may be the difference between survival and victimhood.

I can't talk anyone out of their fear.

I want to caution, though, against making our fears our reality.

What we acquire in our preparedness, we are also emotionally and mentally preparing ourselves to use. If we acquire food? Great, we have enough to share. If we acquire skills and knowledge? Great, we are now a resource for ourselves and others.

But if we acquire weapons? What are we preparing for?

I plan to be the helper. The soft place to land. The voice of calm and reason. I make decisions with the expectation that I am not alone but part of a loving community which—should we be called to—will show up for one another if ever things go sideways.

That is the future and events I plan for.

PART 10

# FAITH, POLITICS, & THE GOLDEN RULE

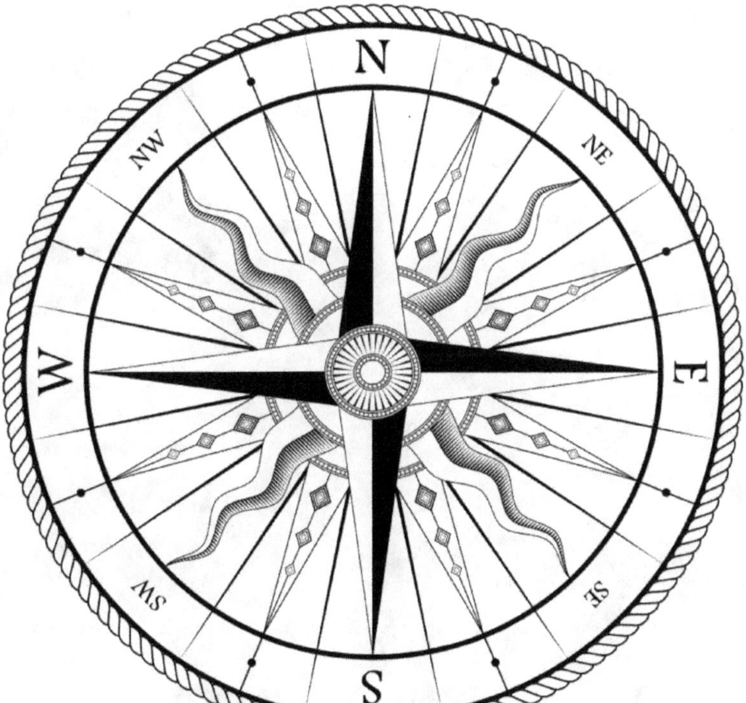

# Chapter 14

## MORALITY, ETHICS, AND FAITH

### WHEN SPIRIT LEADS US

Years ago, my husband, kids, and I had just finished some grocery shopping. As we pulled out of our parking spot to drive toward the exit, I could see an elderly man standing in the lane of traffic outside the store. A couple of cars waited for him to move. One honked impatiently.

I unclipped my seatbelt and told my husband to let me out. Launching myself out of the car, I hurried to the man and asked if he needed help.

He looked at me, eyes wide, and said, "My wife. I've lost my wife!"

He was shaking, with age or nerves I didn't know, and he seemed precarious despite his cane. I waved at the waiting cars to go around us and tried to steer him toward the safety of the sidewalk.

Lost his wife? *Had she died?*

"She was right there, then she was gone. I thought she left. I think she left. I need to find her. I need to find my wife."

*Ah.*

Was she in the grocery store? He thought so. I asked if he knew what she was wearing, he shook his head, growing agitated, so I told him not to worry, I was sure she wouldn't leave without him. I invited him to return to the store with me so that we could have Customer Service call his wife to the service desk. He liked this idea, so we slowly made our way toward the entrance.

But a moment later, a woman rushed out of the store and her face flooded with relief when she saw us. "Oh, thank God!" she said. "Thank you. Thank you so much. I only turned my back for a moment and he was gone. It was only a moment, I swear. He's never done this. Thank you so much."

I assured her he was fine and that I'd been keeping him safe for her.

She grasped the elbow of her beloved and gently guided him back into the store, chiding him for walking off and scaring her.

I returned to my car, took my seat, and as my husband drove toward the exit, a wave of emotion overcame me. I dabbed at the tears that sprang to my eyes and realized that this—*this*—is what love felt like. True, universal, unconditional, hand-of-God type of love.

Before telling my husband to stop and let me out, I remember experiencing a moment's hesitation. We were on our way home, our car loaded with groceries and two bored children. I told myself the man was probably fine and didn't want my help. Was it even my place to intervene? But something in me said, *"Go."*

And I'm grateful that I did, grateful that I listened to that tiny voice inside that urged me to see the humanity of another and act accordingly.

The entire encounter lasted a few minutes before it was over. But inside, I was transformed. I now recognize that not only does every small act hold meaning, but I—*we all*—have the power to embody divine love in this world.

If you ever feel powerless in this life, ponder the many and varied ways you've been the hand of divine love, and let those tears flow. I promise it feels amazing.

## THE UNIVERSAL GOLDEN RULE

- "Do unto others as you would have them do unto you." – Christianity
- "What you yourself hate, do to no [other]." – Judaism
- "Treat others as you would yourself be treated." – Hinduism
- "Hurt not others with that which pains you." – Buddhism
- "Do unto all [people] as you would wish to have done." – Islam
- "Live in harmony, for we are all related." – Native American

(The above edited for gender neutrality. The patriarchy is a topic for another book.)

The Golden Rule exists in some form in religious teachings world-wide. At its core is the presumption that in a world where each individual acts for their own self-interest, there is no morality, but a world in which we act with empathy, we cannot do wrong. When we are connected, it's that much more difficult to act in a way to harm "other" because we would, by extension, be harming our collective selves. At the heart of the universal understanding of ethics, then, is the call to view ourselves as an inseparable part of humankind.

These rules are what most organized religions purport to teach and uphold. Their sacred texts are filled with stories and parables both to guide and to warn and layered atop these basic principles are centuries of tradition and practice and interpretation.

I'm not going to address any of that.

I'm not going to address it not because it's not important to think about and discuss how formal religious practice and institutions often fall victim to the same pitfalls as secular institutions in that those with power or position will often abuse it or seek to retain it at the expense of individual members. I'm not going to address it because there's a more fundamental truth underlying our yearning for a faith practice: trust.

At its core, having faith in someone, some thing, or some creative or spiritual entity or force is our own yearning to trust. We want to trust that our lives matter not just to ourselves but the universe and other living creatures. We want to trust that when we call out for help, there will be an answer. We want to trust that when others act in harmful ways that there will be justice served. We want to trust, because to trust is to have a sense of groundedness, predictability, and meaning to existence. Faith is our willingness and ability to express trust in things that have not yet been borne out in fact.

I trust and have faith that most humans strive to be good people.

I have faith that even when bad things happen to good people that they will not have to suffer alone.

I have faith that even when I don't see the whole picture that there is a collective higher power at work that is moving toward pattern and order and not chaos.

I trust that love, given unconditionally and with my whole heart, is never wasted and always magnified.

I have faith that those who act to harm, belittle, or hoard are not unstoppable, and that loving boundaries are the key to maintaining connection without falling victim to those who might overstep.

I have faith that if enough people act with enough compassion that humanity can achieve great things including its own well-being.

I have faith in the unseen, intangible energies of love and empathy and kindness. I believe that there are truths yet to be understood that make phenomena which appear chaotic, knowable.

I believe in such a thing as life force and souls and that such matters exist beyond the limits of our ability to describe them with language or represent them with physical matter, and I am at peace with the ambiguity and infinite unknowingness of the universe.

And not one of my beliefs infringes on your belief to agree or disagree with me.

And that, my friends, is the Golden Rule in action.

# Chapter 15

## FAITH IS A PRACTICE NOT A DESTINATION

### A HEALTH CRISIS THAT LED TO HEALING

Bear with me on this one, because it will take a moment to get to my point.

Several years ago, my husband had a major medical crisis.

It came on the heels of the pandemic shutdowns during which his primary care physician had retired. By the time he was seen that fateful night in the ER, a concerning medical issue had devolved into crisis.

My husband had known he wasn't well, but because he was afraid of what he might be told, he hadn't wanted to go to the hospital. It took a dear friend, me, and our daughter to convince my husband to be seen.

I don't tell this story to shame him, because who among us has delayed having something checked out? Or put off bringing our car to the garage for that clanking noise just in case it is news we're not ready to hear?

I remember driving to our home, frustrated and scared, trying to convince my husband to seek medical care. I knew he was very,

very ill, and as I looked over at him, I said, "This is *not* the end of our love story."

I wasn't talking about romantic love, so much as *our story*, our partnership, our lives that had somehow spanned decades of raising children, job changes, navigating toxic relationships with other family, the deaths of our parents.

I took him home and let him go to his bedroom to lie down and then called everyone I could think of including the friend who'd urged him to go to the ER.

And twenty minutes later, that dear friend stood in our driveway.

Our friend followed us to the hospital, and all three of us went into the ER. We waited for the doctor in the small examination room, and as they ran tests and treated my husband, this friend stood vigil with me until my husband was discharged the next morning, the sun rising over the horizon.

My husband received a diagnosis none of us were prepared for and suffered more medical setbacks in the weeks and months to follow. But while the journey was emotional and uncertain and at times bleak, from that very first night, we knew we didn't have to walk it alone.

Even when his organs struggled and he'd lost so much weight he needed assistance walking, we had friends, family, and colleagues offering practical and emotional support—meals, prayers, help around our house, hospital equipment, uplifting cards, and shoulders to cry on.

As the months turned into years, my husband dedicated himself to recovery. He'd suffered organ damage and been listed on a transplant list, but while we'd been working hard to keep him as healthy as we could while we waited for the miracle that would keep him with us, we never stopping living.

Forced to take early retirement, he was easily tired but filled with gratitude for the life he still had. He began walking, and at first our progress was measured in yards, not miles. He volunteered a couple of hours a week. We went to performances, out on the lake, and met our kids or friends for dinner or ice cream. We made the plans and kept living as much as his energy level would allow.

I won't claim he's one hundred percent healed, because it's a daily choice to accept that there are limits and still choose to dream beyond them, but this is what I will tell you: at his most recent appointment he was told that they were going to deactivate his transplant listing. No, he wasn't a lost cause. He had healed to the point where the surgery would be riskier than living life.

Three years ago, he received a diagnosis that side-lined him from the future he thought lay before him, but in so doing, we discovered something profound and life-changing.

No matter what this life holds for us, we will never have to face it alone.

And also, I was right. Our love story is far from over. I haven't only been gifted more time with my life partner, I've experienced the best of humanity. I've seen the power of love to carry the light when ours grew dim, and it has only served to strengthen my faith in the inherent goodness of humanity.

Some might note that I didn't credit God or Spirit here, and that's intentional. I hope you will hear me out, because even though I am a part of a faith community, my faith is bigger and more complex than a single entity, because my faith is inclusive, expansive, and as simple as this: love.

In my mind God is love, and love is the collective, uplifting, empowering, healing, compassionate force of all creation. We, as humans, are a part of that collective love. And when we show up for one another? We are God's hands at work.

## SEPARATING FAITH FROM INSTITUTIONAL BELIEFS AND TRADITIONS

---

*The love of the universe has no body.*
*We must be the eyes that see injustice,*
*the ears that hear cries of suffering,*
*the hands which offer aid and comfort,*
*the hearts which beat in a united rhythm,*
*the lungs to breathe in collective hope,*
*the legs to walk away from hate, and*
*the elbows to link in solidarity of purpose.*

---

Separate from any belief in a specific religious practice or institution, I believe in the collective power of humanity to be the light, love, comfort, and hope for one another. We are literally called to this role in every major religion through the many-colored versions of the Golden Rule. The beauty of this view is that it doesn't require any of us to adhere to a specific faith practice to be loving humans to one another, nor does it reject a belief in a higher divine power.

Yes, many of us find comfort in calling upon the memory of Jesus or the power of Allah, and I understand and respect that. But if we strip away the various and varied institutional beliefs and traditions and get to the core message—the love—we can see a universal standard of moral and ethical behavior based in compassion and generosity.

But what if what I would want for myself differs from what you might want for yourself? What then? How do we apply the Golden Rule when we don't view the world from the same perspective?

We can add a corollary to this basic law based in empathy: If I want something different for myself than someone else would want for themselves, then the moral thing for me to do is to take their feelings and views into account.

The Golden Rule is grace in action. It is about building and fostering connection and goodwill between people. Imposing my will on another or excluding them based on my belief system is not in keeping with the intent of this universal law.

More fundamentally—if we pull way, way back from any individual decision—the goal at the root of any version of the Golden Rule is to foster connection between people. If my actions are divisive or serve to deny someone else happiness, health, or autonomy, then those actions would generally be deemed morally wrong. If my actions are to do something which *you would not choose for yourself* (sexual orientation, gender identity, friends or loved ones of another skin color or religion) then the moral thing to do is to allow me to choose freely without your outside interference—a freedom to choose for myself—what you would choose if our roles were reversed.

Mind blown yet? Are the philosophers ready to come for me yet? Well, hold on, because I'm about to ruffle some more feathers.

I would posit, that at the root of most bigotry, racism, othering, misogyny, and religious intolerance, are practices in stark contrast to the core teachings in every major religion. Should your religious practice encourage you to impose your will onto others against their desires or if it encourages division instead of inclusion, these are practices and traditions to take a long, hard look at. They seem, to my eye, more about human power than divine love.

## MOVING FROM FEAR TO FAITH: HOW TRAUMA NARROWS OUR FOCUS AND SILOS US

I was talking to my husband one recent morning, and I'll tell you that I don't know what the present looks like as you're reading this, but our present? Right now? Pretty damn chaotic and terrifying. Anyway, my husband said, "I'm feeling calmer today, but just barely, I don't know how you do it." He looked over at me.

I felt compassion for my husband. When the world feels unpredictable, it brings up a trauma response he carries from childhood. He's now aware of it and is working through it, but when that anxiety is triggered, like happens for so many of us, he has to fight the pull that says that he's the only one that can save himself, soothe himself, or whose "help" he can count on.

If that resonates with you, you may be carrying your own trauma. But whether you're aware of triggers or have run-of-the-mill (!) anxiety, it can be difficult to get out of the racing-thoughts head-space and back into your physical body.

In Chapter 22 I talk about strategies for grounding and recentering ourselves which can help in emotional regulation, but beyond grounding and breathing exercises, it can help to put our anxiety into a visual context.

I told my husband that when I'm anxious, it narrows my worldview and focus so that it's like I'm looking at the world through a tube. I'm hyper-fixated on the problem directly in front of me and it looks huge and scary. I find myself feeling isolated with only my own experiences and resources to call upon.

But the tube? That is our anxiety limiting our worldview. It is our trauma response telling us that we're alone and that the options available are limited to what our perspective allows us to see. But what if we paused, took a breath, and allowed ourselves to let the tube limiting our view disappear? We may well see a host of people nearby ready to give a hand, offer their own perspective on the way forward, or able to share resources and ideas.

When I say I have faith in things being not as dire as they appear, it is me saying, despite the narrow view my anxiety is showing me, that I trust there is a larger picture I'm not seeing but which exists. I have only to let go of my fear to see what possibilities lay before me.

# Chapter 16

## POLITICS *IS* PERSONAL

Several years ago I was chatting with friends about openly discussing politics in today's social climate. They wondered why I would want to, given how ugly and contentious it often becomes. I told them that engaging on hot-topics helps me practice my tolerance–like any skill, it feels easier when exercised consistently. It gets me out of my own self-validating bubble and helps me understand others who, by and large, feel just as passionately about their point of view.

But, if these discussions rarely change anyone's mind, why bother to "enter the fray" at all?

Years ago when I was but a fresh-faced college student, I stood waiting at a bus stop with a handful of others. An older woman ambled down the sidewalk. We all shifted to allow her room to pass, but at the moment she came abreast of me, she whirled toward me, cursing, flailing her arm angrily, and spat: "YOU GET OUT OF HERE! WE DON'T WANT ANY OF YOUR KIND AROUND HERE! YOU HEAR ME? GET OUT! GET OUT OF HERE!!!"

I backed away at her continued abuse, darting glances at my fellow bus-stop crowd, because, obviously, I did not know this woman, she did not know me, and yet for some reason in her mind, I was *the enemy.*

It may sound insignificant as stories go. How much harm could an elderly homeless woman do to a 19-year-old at a bus stop in broad daylight? The bus soon arrived, I climbed aboard, and we headed to campus.

But the tears came only when one of the handful of people who'd witnessed this exchange touched my arm and said, "She's not right in the head. She didn't mean that for you." And I realized, that what I needed most in that bizarre, hate-filled, unfairly targeted moment was someone to acknowledge that they saw, and they recognized it was not right, and none of that hate-filled rant was okay. What that compassionate woman gave me–even though she likely felt as powerless as I did to change the misdirected hate in that old woman's mind–was the knowledge that I wasn't alone, sometimes people are hurtful, and we don't have to pretend it's normal or okay.

Which is my long-winded way of saying that sometimes when we talk about hot-topic issues, it's not that we believe it'll change hearts and minds with mere words, it's because there may be someone out there who needs to know they have an ally. They need one person to say:

I see you.

You're not alone.

Sometimes people are hurtful.

You don't have to pretend it's okay.

## CANCEL CULTURE AND LEARNING TO TALK ABOUT THE HARD STUFF

---

*In personal relationships and politics, remember:*
*don't ever trade your voice for*
*power or privilege.*
*In the end you'll lose both.*
*Your voice* is *your power.*
*Collectively, our voices can change the world.*

---

As of the writing of this book, my country has experienced enormous cultural, social, and political division. It's so pervasive, it seems the one and only topic on the news or social media, but for many the adage "never discuss politics or religion" has been drilled into them since birth.

It's not uncommon for someone to want to speak about topics which feel very important and personal only to be shushed and told that religion and politics have no place in polite society and such discussions only cause strife in friendships, on social media, or at the dinner table.

Yet, what are politics, and religion for that matter, but our values and beliefs codified and applied? Are they not both, in their own way, the framework we agree to allow ourselves and our actions to be governed or judged? And, if our beliefs are deemed antithetical to our friends, neighbors, coworkers and more, then why on earth would we be spending time hanging out with these people? If we aren't granted the freedom to speak of those issues which weigh heavy upon our hearts or that ignite our passions and define our humanity, are we really seeking meaningful connection with others or parallel, but distinct paths of existence?

I'm going to suggest that when we tell others they shouldn't speak about such matters, our concerns are less about decorum and conflict and more about our own unwillingness to listen and provide space for thoughts and opinions which don't align with our own. We should seek not to silence ourselves or others, but to foster genuine conversation about how we each came to believe or stand for positions that appear so opposed. It is only in genuine conversation, conducted with respect and curiosity, that we will find our way through the apparent divisions to new communities of understanding.

When we deny ourselves permission to speak freely and openly about politics or religion it is another way in which our society tells us to bury our feelings. Buried feelings, though, have a tendency to rear their ugly heads in unhealthy ways whether through self-harming behaviors or acting out. I should think it more desirable to allow for honest discussion, wouldn't you?

Rather than stifle ourselves and others, it would be better to practice open-hearted listening. It would be preferable to allow ourselves and those around us to be in a space of sharing our deepest vulnerabilities and values. If we aren't comfortable with honest discussion, we must ask ourselves whether living in denial is preferable to whatever consequence our truths might elicit?

## ALL THE COLORS OF THE RAINBOW

Speaking of speaking our truths… it always surprises me that there are people who can look around at the vibrant and varied world we live in—see all the species and colors and permutations which exist—and then claim that some arbitrary piece or vantage point within creation is superior to another. Our natural world is not binary but measured by degrees and spectrums. To claim that some feature or facet or outward expression is the "right" way to exist and to ignore the many wonderful points of light up and down the spectrum of human experience is to trap us all in a monochromatic world. Make no mistake: whether we are speaking of the color of our skin, those we are attracted to, or how we identify ourselves, the choice to "other" anyone is about control, not morals.

Shame is a tool society uses to discourage unwelcome behaviors. It's not wrong in and of itself. We shame people for picking their noses, because it's gross and can spread illness, and frankly I'm all for that kind of social correction. But when shame is used against people for being their authentic selves—for merely daring to exist—it's no longer a tool of correction, but one of control and exclusion. When we shame people for being born with the "wrong" color skin or for feeling love for the "wrong" people, we are using shame as a weapon, not a tool.

Are they picking their noses in public? No? *Then let them be.*

## SEPARATING THE STAR FROM THEIR POLITICS

It's rarely a good idea to idolize anyone, all of us being fallible creatures, but it's particularly tricky if that someone is some sort of public figure. We can never really know a celebrity, influencer, artist, or politician beyond what they reveal to us. We've never seen the parts of their homes they haven't curated and cleaned for a photo shoot, met them in the hallway when they haven't had enough sleep, or had an honest and private chat about their fears and dreams. When we idolize anyone, they can do no wrong in our eyes, and we, in turn, lose the ability to criticize them or to hold them accountable. Idolatry gives another the power to abuse our starry-eyed adoration to their own end.

No, it is much better to admire people for their actions—to note their achievements and talents—than to view them as perfect.

We have all seen how high-profile people who have built entire fandoms can, with a single social media post or public comment, break the hearts of all who ever resonated with their work. I get it! It's difficult to absorb that an entertainer or artist whose work we've enjoyed holds views antithetical to our own.

It's okay to struggle with that, and in an increasingly polarized world with instantaneous messaging, it's easy to find something to be both up-in-arms about and to have it spread like wildfire. In those situations, it's okay to pause and think about whatever is news to our ears. Is this outright hate-speech or merely a different or competing viewpoint I might respect even if I don't agree? Is the action something from the past they've learned and grown from or an ongoing character flaw we've chosen not to see? Do we burn all the albums, books, or what-not we have ever bought or simply decide not to give this particular creator any more of our money or attention?

Maybe that creator has already offered a public apology. Maybe they have doubled-down. Someday that creator may see how wrong they were. Or maybe they won't. Maybe the sting of any particular insult we feel will dissipate with time or perhaps it will solidify our new, lowered opinion.

There are no wrong answers here, because your feelings, whatever they may be, are valid.

But, here is something I want you to consider: It's okay to love the art, the work, the creation and not love the creator. When I write a book, I write it for myself first, but once I publish it? It is *yours*. What you experience when you read it? You *own* that. Whatever joy or freedom or sense of being seen? That comes from the universe and lives within you—the creator was simply the conduit. We can love the water and feel ambivalent about the pipes it runs through. We can find the storms terrifying, but the flowers that bloom after? Those are ours to enjoy.

It can be very hard to separate the star from their politics or views, but consider that if you feel somehow a target or dismissed or minimized by some creator's views, wouldn't it be the ultimate in rebellious courage to decide that *you* get to decide how you feel about it? *Because you do.*

PART 11

# WHO AM I?

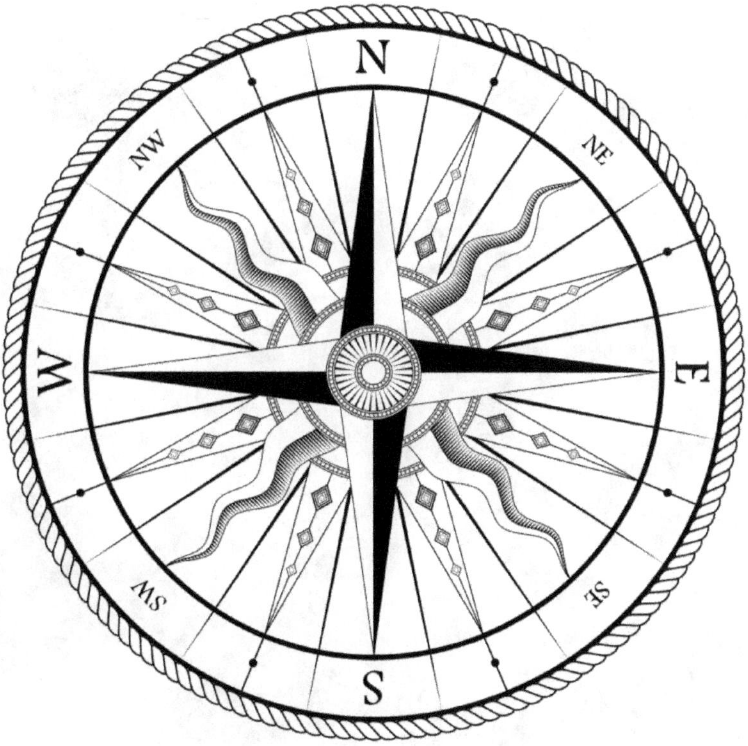

# Chapter 17

## WHO AM I?

### DECORATING FOR LIFE

This may seem an odd place to begin a section on identity, but think of it as me working from the outside in.

How many of us have driven down dark roads and peered into people's homes to see how they are decorated? <sheepishly raises hand> How many of us have walked into someone's space for the first time and been struck by how "them" it feels… or doesn't?

Our homes are a reflection of our state of mind, an outward expression of what we find meaningful and aesthetically pleasing, and a first impression for those we are newly in relationship with. In short: our homes are telling on us!

This is why so many realtors recommend sanitizing our homes when we put them on the market so potential buyers can see themselves living there rather than find space among the seller's memories. But while it's still our home, shouldn't it feel like it? I'm endlessly puzzled by people who treat their home like a stranger instead of an extension of themselves.

There are entire industries built on home decorating, garden design, and renovation how-to. There's no need to copy someone else's decor or live in the equivalent of a model rental unit devoid of personal expression. This is no time to be aspirational (I'm looking at you, white couches) but authentic and honest. Function and practicality can still be attractive. Our homes should work with our lifestyle and personal needs. We will be most comfortable in a home that, for lack of a better word, feels like *home.*

When my kids were in their first apartments, we made mood boards and then went on the hunt for treasures that fit. Décor doesn't have to be expensive. I've known many who have proudly revamped their space with thrift shop finds and freecycle scores.

If the idea of decorating overwhelms you, find a friend who loves this sort of thing. I will never forget spending hours in a paint store with a friend who had to choose colors for every room of her house so the builder could move forward. She was overwhelmed. I was thrilled to help! Once over that hurdle, she was more excited to fill those spaces with her own finds and make them her own.

I like to decorate with multi-purpose pieces of furniture—items that can be used as a coffee table or a side table, or the roller cart that can serve as a mini-island or a casual eating spot—which allow for reinventing my spaces to suit my needs over time.

Now, I have thoughts on the whole "neutrals" aesthetic. Yes, absolutely, in a small space, a neutral décor or backdrop opens things visually, and neutrals are calming. But, so are ocean blues, soft greens, and the warm and rusty hues of nature. Black and white makes a bold statement, but so do the rainbow of colors of tropical birds and sun-loving flowers. My point is, we live in a world of color and too often feel we aren't allowed to wallow in our favorite hues. If that orange throw pillow is speaking to you? Get it. It will make you smile every time you see it, guaranteed.

As a woman who has painted a TV armoire dusky purple and has happily enjoyed a row of storage cabinets in deep bluegrass green, whose living room currently boasts shades of robin's egg blue mixed with burnt orange, I am giving you permission to make your space uniquely and beautifully and unequivocally *yours.* Mix and match. Collect over time. Don't copy a perfectly curated magazine ad from a single retailer, but infuse your environment with memories and photographs, and hues that make you feel energized, rested, loved, and happy. Don't simply copy trends; be inspired by them.

The one piece of advice I give to everyone starting out in a new home is: invest in original art. This may seem odd, but I have reasons. Way back when I was newly married, I would often stop in at a small art gallery (conveniently located next to the Chinese food restaurant). One day I happened upon a beautiful watercolor still-life on rice paper. I loved everything about this piece and came to revisit it often. Finally, even though it was more than I felt I could justify spending on a piece of décor, I decided I was going to buy it.

They wrapped it carefully in brown paper, and I brought it home. I'd never owned anything so fancy, and I loved how unique it was. It hangs above my mantel to this day. Every time I look at it, I know that no one else has this exact painting, that it is mine alone. I think about the artist and how happy they must have been to sell their creative work.

Original art—folk, painting, sculpture, etc.—is an investment in both another's creativity and our own aesthetic. If it is our own art or that of a loved one, so much the better!

Ultimately, know that paint can be repainted. Items can be re-thrifted. Our space can and should evolve with us, but unless we plan to sell our home or move in the near future, it makes so much sense to make our homes the sanctuaries in our existence instead of having them simply be the waiting rooms of life.

Our environments affect our mood and reflect our emotional state. Be intentional. Be creative. Have fun. Make your space a home.

## LIVING AN AUTHENTIC LIFE

In my high school senior yearbook, out of one-hundred-eighty-something graduates, I was voted "Most Serious". It has always befuddled me, this distinction, because my friends and family knew that while, yes, I was studious and shy, I was also someone who loved dry humor, being silly—heck, I danced in the rain on hot summer days! More than once! Who was this "serious" person they spoke of?

It wasn't until recently that I realized it wasn't a failure or misjudgment on the part of the yearbook committee. If they didn't see me as anything other than "serious" it said less about their perception and more about how I felt safe being perceived. To be honest, they didn't know the real me, because I didn't show the real me to many people. I was afraid to be my authentic self, back then, so how could they know how *unlike* the *real* me that moniker was?

I know that—back then—I was insecure, socially awkward, naïve, and desperate not to draw attention to myself. I'd been relentlessly bullied in younger days, and while I'd grown to know and feel safe with my core group of friends, I was wary and, yes, judgmental of anyone who appeared to be playing for an audience of the popular ones. I didn't trust them, because I knew they didn't trust themselves, and I was careful not to reveal anything that might highlight an insecurity that could be used against me. Basically, I was like almost every other teen.

As insecure, wounded beings, most of us spend our formative years (and even young adulthood) guarded and shy or loud and daring, with both states of being designed to mask the vulnerabilities within us. What time and distance has revealed is that authenticity *is* power. It is grounding and, yes, even attractive.

---

*Celebrate your strengths and admit to your faults. Leading an authentic life—warts and all—takes power away from those who would manipulate through shame.*

---

It's not easy to reach a state of self-validation and acceptance, but it's what I hope each of us can achieve, because it brings such peace.

There's an old saying: "Everyone grows more conservative with age." I would argue that that is a myth. Yes, some people do grow more conservative. But the truth I see is that as we age, we usually become more ourselves. Whatever our tendencies or formative or transformative experiences might be, as we age, the sheen of social compliance and willingness to conform begin to wear off. We become more ourselves in values, in outward appearance, and in manner. This isn't meant to say that there is no choice in the matter. There is definite room to lean into qualities we want to enhance or grow and lean away from those that may not serve us, but part of the joy of aging is not apologizing for being or becoming our authentic selves.

If we have always loved to laugh loudly, we will seek out those who enjoy the sound of laughter. If we want to enrich our minds with philosophical discussions about life, the universe, and everything, we can seek out like-minded souls with which to explore those topics. We will become more emotionally and spiritually connected to our communities because they will reflect back to us our authentic selves, free of artifice or the need to hide some aspect of our truth.

What I describe, though, is a healthy environment. If you find yourself going inward more and more, expressing greater amounts of fear about the outside world or those within it, or find yourself feeling anger or anxiety as your primary emotions, then you are likely not in a space where you feel safe to be your authentic self.

What if, however, and hear me out, the person you've become isn't pleasant to be around? Have you found those around you distancing themselves, calling you close-minded, hurtful, self-centered, or angry? Are *you* the person others have gone "no contact" with?

It's not an easy task to consider that maybe the person we've become is someone even we wouldn't want to spend time with. But the hard truth is that who we become is a matter of free will. How we respond to every hardship, trauma, or insult in this life is a choice. Whether we experience pain or loss or insult is a matter of chance, but our response? That's all on us.

We can become angry, or hardened, or protective—all natural and understandable responses. But what if we fight injustice by becoming more empathetic? What if, when we see the dark sides of humanity, we become more determined to hold the light and hope for others? What if, instead of closing ourselves off, we show that vulnerability in the form of authenticity robs those who would try to manipulate or lesson us of their power?

We have the choice to celebrate ourselves and others, to build communities of those who will love every quirky, colorful, thoughtful, exuberant aspect of us. To do otherwise is to build a cage for ourselves and lock it from the inside.

One last thought on being "authentic". We in the community of "love and light" often throw around the phrase "shine your light!" Which is, yes, intended to encourage others to live their truth, be their own sparkly, glittery, out-of-the-norm unique splendiferous selves. But, there's another side to that phrase. Shining our light should begin with illuminating our true selves. What is it that we might be hoping to keep hidden? *Why* do we want to hide that aspect of ourselves? Who are we afraid will see it? Answering those questions and becoming comfortable "in the limelight" allows us to live with authenticity and without shame, because shame is often at the root of those dark aspects of ourselves we hope to hide from view or project onto others.

Is it *our* shame or shame directed at us from society? Who in society and for what purpose? Shame isn't a natural sensation but one created and enforced within a society. Once we understand this, it becomes easier to see it as the artificial creation of those who wish to control others. So, understanding that, we can shine that light, acknowledge and deal with those places we wanted to formerly keep in shadow, and become free to live openly, freely, joyfully, lumpy bumpy bobbly bits and all. We can redirect or reflect that shame back to its origins where it can be addressed by the creator and not absorbed by us.

## ACT YOUR AGE AND OTHER NONSENSE

I feel like I'm burying the lede here, so I hope you are paying attention. There are a lot of things we humans do to keep other humans in neat, easily understood boxes. Shame is one of them. Expectations of behavior or dress or myths that assume we become "more conservative with age" are all designed to make other people more predictable. When they dare to behave differently, we label them the problem, not our rigid expectations.

But these expectations are our own doing, our own insufferable closemindedness, our own inability or unwillingness to open ourselves or worldview in accepting that as we all seek to live our happiest, truest, best lives, *so do others*. And what's more? They are allowed to!

Maybe we ourselves feel the weight of shame or judgment or societal constraints and feel triggered or upset when we see others are choosing not to be governed by the same rules. How dare they? But that's an *us* problem, not a *them* problem.

Not long ago we shamed children for being left-handed. We as a society forced conformity, because they dared to be born with a certain preference. This is true world-wide. Nowadays most of us recognize that this is a ridiculous thing to be focused on. What harm does it do anyone if another is born with a preference for a different dominant hand than the majority? No amount of punitive measures or shame has changed the number of children born left-handed (roughly ten percent), but we have finally, as a society (I hope!), come to accept that that is just how some people are.

Think about that for a moment.

We have chosen to stop shaming people for being left-handed. We have chosen to reject beliefs that left-handedness is unlucky, a sign of dishonesty, or a lack of intelligence.

We can *choose* not to shame people for being born with certain preferences. We can *choose* to be accepting.

Other people are allowed to wear their hair a certain way, love who they want to love in an adult and consenting manner, express themselves in words or actions or identify and name themselves however they so choose so long as it does not take away another's right to do the same.

---

*People have a right to be who they want to be so long as it does not take away another's right to do the same.*

---

Even if they have a hate-speech tattoo or choose to be in a sexual or romantic relationship that is antithetical to what we would choose for ourselves, they have the right to make that choice and as a result *so do you.* Another person's choice to dress a certain way, speak a certain way, use certain words or enter into consensual relation with another has zero impact on my choices. I can choose to be offended, but that is also my choice. Frankly, I choose, as the popular advice goes to *let them*. It is what I would want for myself.

## IS HONESTY THE BEST POLICY?

A byproduct of living an authentic life is this sense that we don't hide our true thoughts and opinions.

I'll never forget the moment my mother finished reading my very first manuscript. She loved romances and had read them for decades, so I knew she understood what a reader of the genre expected. I also knew my draft was rough—it was a first draft after all—but as an aspiring author I needed to know my writing had promise.

"Well?" I said, prepared to admit to its flaws but awaiting some glimmer of encouragement.

"It's fine," she said. "A bit predictable."

I pretended to be okay, acknowledging that I had work to do, but I was crushed.

I'd completed a goal I'd set for myself of finishing a manuscript. I'd written for hours and days with a newborn asleep in her donut pillow on my lap when I could have been napping, too. I'd written and rewritten and jotted ideas, the characters coming to life in my mind for the first time, and it had been a thrilling, exciting, vulnerable process, because as much as my characters weren't *me,* they were also all of me—my biases, my dreams and my worldview. Their life on paper was a dream realized.

What my pragmatic and honest-to-a-painful-fault mother didn't understand is that I wasn't looking for her to tell me it was ready for primetime. I wasn't even looking for her suggestions on where the story could be improved. I was seeking a congratulations on my effort and a tidbit of "I like this one aspect of what you did here" note of encouragement.

I learned a few things that day. One, your family, as much as they love you, may not always understand your dreams. Your mother/sister/friend is not necessarily your editor. And, sometimes, the honest truth is brutal.

In the end, I revised the every-loving-stuffing out of that first manuscript. The version I eventually sent off to an editor at a major publishing house was ultimately rejected, but the letter from that editor was everything I'd hoped to receive from my mother. It specified ways in which my writing showed promise, gave me constructive feedback for improvement, and motivated me to continue as he encouraged me to submit my next project.

Years later, when my mother finally purchased my debut book (my fourth manuscript at this point), she later told me she'd rated it 4/5 stars, because no book is perfect and, as a reader, she didn't trust those 5-star ratings anyway. <sigh>

That's a tangent from the topic at hand, though. Because the real question is what should my mother have said? Everyone has heard Sir Walter Scott's famous quote: "Oh, what a tangled web we weave, when first we practice to deceive." It speaks to the difficulty of keeping up with a lie. But what of the little white lies or lies of omission which all of us have at one point or another engaged in? Are these moments where we stretch the truth to get over hurting someone's feelings a kindness or a cop-out? Are we not remaining our authentic selves when we gloss over our "truths" to be kind to others?

At the time, my mother's blunt and unsoftened manner felt harsh, but I know that she was proud of me for pursuing my dreams and bought every book I wrote, even though they weren't her preferred sub-genre.

The interaction showed me that, as much as I loved that woman, I'd need to seek out others to bolster my ego. It also highlighted for me the importance of compassionate authenticity. It's okay to speak and own our truth, particularly if we feel unheard or sidelined by others. But, if our "truth" is simply our perspective or opinion? We need to tread lightly. There is nothing inauthentic about compassion, sensitivity, and being a loving cheerleader to others.

PART 12

# WHY AM I HERE?

# Chapter 18

## YOUR PURPOSE AND PASSION(S)

### FOLLOW YOUR "OOOOOHS"

I get it. You might say only those with privilege can pursue their heart's desire. Only those who don't have to think about safety-nets and logistics and finances can follow their dreams. Do you believe that? Because I don't.

Pursuing one's passions in this life is definitely something made *easier* in certain circumstances than in others, but even those in the most difficult of circumstances manage to find their voice in art, dance, music, and literature.

That's what I think about when I think about what it means to find your passion: it means finding your unique voice, expressing your unique perspective. Whether you express yourself through art or find a way to contribute to humanity in a more hands-on manner, when you are doing *the thing* whatever it may be, you feel electrified, purpose-filled, joyous. Life seems to have meaning and make sense.

We can enjoy lots of things but passion is a calling. It's that something that gives us purpose and makes our soul feel alive. Your passion isn't about the action of writing or the playing of the violin. It's what you *do* with that skill and the reasons you do it.

Passion can feel elusive, too, when we are distracted by all the noise around us and the often strong and overbearing voices which tell us what we should want and should do.

So how does one find their passion, their calling, their purpose? First of all, I firmly believe we can have multiple "callings," often they will dovetail with one another, or follow in happy succession, but here are several thoughts for being able to see them:

1) **Your calling will call to you.** You'll find yourself being drawn back to and interested in "the thing" regardless of where you are in life, how much money you have, and whether you get paid for doing it. It might be writing. It might be studying the skies. It might be dance, or physics, or music, or fixing things or building things or caring for people or animals or… you get the idea. It's often something we did as children before we were told to do something more lucrative or important. It's something we find ourselves returning to as we move through life.

2) **You will self-adjust toward it.** Throughout studies or jobs, follow your "oohs—the path that excites you whether or not it's the path you expected to be on. Even if the path seems to not directly lead to your destination, as long as you are moving in the general direction, keep pursuing it.

3) **It will provide its own fulfillment.** The path may, but does not have to, include recognition or value to anyone else. This is important, because the voices of others frequently get in the way of seeing what we want for ourselves. We

should enjoy "the thing" even without accolades. We should feel a pull to do it even if no one ever knew it was us doing it.

4) **Your calling will feel natural not forced.** Be careful to discern between anxiety (the thing we feel we should be doing) and excitement (the thing we want to do.) If you feel you have to justify or talk yourself into a path, it's not the right path for you at this time. Your purpose isn't a "should" so much as an "if only I could."

It's an interesting theme in every fiction story I have written that one or both of the characters are on a path of self-discovery and looking for that thing in life that makes them feel they've found their purpose. Our passions, I firmly believe, are our souls remembering what we were sent here to do. And the beautiful thing about passions is that they can come to fruition in their own perfect timing. They were a seed our souls planted before we were born, and sometimes they bloom early, and sometimes those seedlings take a decades-long meandering journey before revealing themselves.

Those "oohs" we sometimes feel? Those are moments when we get that sense that *this* path, *these* conditions, *this* environment or *these* people will help us grow. Those "oohs" are signs to make micro-adjustments in how much light we get, how much water, whether we are challenged or pruned to toughen our stalks or grow more directly into our purpose.

Passions are layered and a soul can have more than one, and sometimes? They dovetail with other parts of our lives or people who've entered our orbit in ways we cannot see as anything other than divine timing, kismet, or "meant to be."

Never view the small things which bring us joy as inconsequential. The individual that is fascinated by the tiny details of some obscure interest may hold the key to unlocking something incredibly profound for humanity simply because they were called to pause, take notice, and look upon something with a driven curiosity.

Perhaps there is a pastime you engage in which brings you a simple joy. Whether it's hiking in nature, fiber arts, gaming design, talking to your pet with silly voices, collecting rocks, decorating, reading a favorite genre, cooking, carpentry, skating, or any of the thousands upon thousands of niche or common occupations we humans engage in, that very thing is important and has purpose.

Perhaps you make a thing you then gift to others. Perhaps you provide for a safe or inviting or sturdy home environment for yourself and family. Perhaps you care for those with less in a way that brings them dignity and companionship, or you organize events or fundraisers or people because being in purposeful community with others brings you joy. Perhaps you entertain or give emotional respite to others. All of these things matter and all of them are ways in which we humans live this human experience in ways which make us happy and self-fulfilled.

Anyone who tells you that doing so is selfish or a waste of time is missing out on what it means to be alive. Don't let anyone steal your joy or tell you that following your bliss is a silly pipe dream.

You matter and because you matter, what you *do* matters. All of it. The big things we feel drawn and called to doing and the small things like dancing in our pajamas like no one is watching. You have this one life—a mixed up jumble of good things and really, really hard things. And if you've been listening and not skipping chapters, you'll know you can set boundaries, and run toward green flags, and keep turning yourself in the direction of your own personal *oohs*… or not. But those are choices. Every moment is a choice.

I know what choice I'm making.

## IT'S NOT A JOB; IT'S AN OPPORTUNITY

It might feel difficult to differentiate between the things we are good at and what we might refer to as a calling, purpose, or passion.

Loosely, those things we feel good at are externally validated or quantifiable. So, it's something others would notice and potentially reward. This is independent of how the activity makes us *feel*. We can be good at something and not feel passionate about it.

Our passions? They are their own reward. They feed and fulfill something inside of us. It may not be something we can articulate or even that other people tend to value. But pursuing the passions in our life? They will bring opportunity, they will, eventually, help us find our "tribe" of like-minded people, and they will carry us through the times where the outside world isn't validating us because they are their own reward.

## GROWING OLD, GROWING UP, OR SIMPLY GROWING?

I began this chapter speaking to passion(s), because many of us will have multiple throughout our lives or ones which evolve with time. I highly recommend to new parents in particular that they reserve room in their lives for hobbies and interests outside of the marriage or child-rearing. Why? Because child-rearing is an action and it may even feel like a calling, but it is finite. When that child begins school or graduates or moves out and you are asked to let go, I want you to have something to turn to with the sense of "finally!" I want you eager to throw yourself toward that inner calling you've been dabbling at or pushing to the side. I want you excited to throw yourself into your next chapter in life with enthusiasm as you grow yourself now that you've grown your children.

The same message applies to those approaching retirement. Those years, God willing, after you quit the day job or career are open to possibility. What are your plans for them? What will you create? Who will you connect with? Where will you go? Dream for yourself. Never stop growing, learning, striving, connecting. You have skills and experience the world is clamoring for. Live this next phase of your life as if you have been chomping at the bit for this time.

We have, hopefully, learned that we are able to wear many hats in this life and they don't always define us and can be switched out as we grow or seek to try a new one on for size. One life: many hats.

## FEELING STUCK – OVERCOMING STAGNATION/INERTIA

Sure, 'one life, many hats' feels like a catchy phrase, but what if we've worn a hat so long it is comfortable and familiar even if it no longer suits or we're tired of it? What happens when we feel stuck?

What if we dreamed the thing, got the degree, made the connections, did the work, and we're tired or no longer inspired? What then?

Two things: feeling stuck is often a result of waiting for something external to change—for someone to make a decision or for the environment to feel "right." My advice is: never leave your forward momentum in someone else's hands. You have a book on submission? *Great*. Now write something else while you wait.

Secondly, you may feel that you're stuck, because the excitement of doing the thing has waned. You've stagnated. You might have done this thing you felt called to do so long, you've lost sight of the reward you thought you'd get, it no longer feels like much of a reward, or you simply feel stale.

All of that's valid, but it points to either forgetting why you started the thing or feeling that you are no longer growing. Go back and write down the reasons you felt called to do the thing you're doing. Are they still valid? Are there new reasons? If you feel you've stopped growing and are only making more widgets in the same mold as when you began, perhaps you now feel called to mentor others in your area of expertise. Become the teacher. Pass the baton.

Perhaps this passion has run its course. That, too, can happen. If so, you are in an exciting space! Follow your curiosity wherever it may lead. Take a class. Sign up for something new. Reach out to an old friend you lost touch with. Explore this space of possibility and consider that perhaps you are not stuck or stagnating but simply in a space of rest before taking action again.

# Chapter 19

## EMPLOYMENT

### WORKING FOR A LIVING

There are countless books and resources on how to find your calling, get a foot in the door, make your application stand-out, and start your own business. This book is none of those things. What I will say is I've done warehouse work, waitressed, held administrative jobs and managerial positions, worked for a one-person employer, a charitable organization, an international corporation, and for myself. The take-home message I have is this: know your worth. Not only in terms of the going rate for the tasks you are performing but as a human deserving respect and compassion. Know that any of us can do something we hate for a finite amount of time but that that same task becomes soul-sucking if there is no end in sight. Know that everyone you meet has a life outside of where they earn their paycheck and that it is both none of your business and incumbent on each of us to give space and grace for that life to exist.

Don't be afraid to ask for what you want and insist on getting what you need. Know the difference between the two so you know your own boundaries.

Never put up with abuse from anyone for any reason. Not even for a job. Your self-worth demands nothing less.

Make goals that exist outside of work. Unless you are fortunate enough to "do what you love" then you are working in exchange for an income. That income buys you food, shelter, entertainment, and more. Those are where your goals lie. It's never just about the money, so don't let it become so.

## WORK/LIFE BALANCE

Those people who make a five-year, ten-year, twenty-year plan? Yeah, I've not met them either. But the idea behind it? I'm all for it. I'm all for dreaming about the things we are working toward so we align the time and energy we are expending today with the goals we want to achieve down the road.

But that "down the road" focus ignores that most of us are living right here in the present. Today we can dream about that ten-year milestone, but if it comes at the cost of nine years of grueling single-mindedness, is the cost worth the achievement?

Goals are fantastic for keeping us from stagnating or veering off course, and revisiting them from time to time helps us incorporate new information or realities. But don't ever forget that this moment right here and now is the last time we have to live it.

Now it's gone.

And just like that, we might spend years looking down the road without realizing that the small moments—every minute which passes—is as worthy of our attention and gratitude as that big thing on the distant horizon.

This is why it is so important to balance the time and energy we invest in our employment with the life outside of work that makes that employment necessary.

You might tell yourself you are earning and saving for your child's higher education, but if you miss every sporting event, family vacation, or shared meal along the way, will you even have a relationship by then?

The reality may be that you have to work long hours, extra shifts, or an offset schedule just to make finances and logistics work. Maybe you come home and the last thing you want to do is engage in conversation, cook a meal, or help your kids with their homework. I see you. I get it.

I will only say this: your struggle is your family's struggle whether you want to admit it or not. Be honest with what your needs are. Maybe you need a few minutes to decompress and maybe that means sitting in silence, playing a video game, or walking in to a clean kitchen so you can prepare a simple dinner. When families lean on one another for support, that's life. That's shared responsibility and care.

The "life balance" piece might be asking for a revised schedule to accommodate your kids' games or medical appointments. It might be letting go of some of the "shoulds" so that you can get to the "wants". It might be as simple as making time once a week or once a month or whenever the heck you can to go for a walk, visit a park or museum, engage in a hobby or puzzle, or gather in the kitchen once every couple of weeks to spend a few hours batch-cooking meals.

One final word: unpaid work is still work. For every person who has raised children, kept a household running, organized repairs and appointments, driven kids and relatives and elderly neighbors for shopping or medical care or sporting events, cared for pets or livestock, tended a vegetable garden, nursed someone back to health, organized family events, bought and wrapped group gifts, cooked meals for more than themselves, they know this already. These tasks are work whether we are paid an hourly wage or not. If we are taking on a greater proportion of these tasks and our spouse or partner isn't acknowledging our work and providing for appropriate balance, this can (and likely will) lead to resentment.

So, I bring things full circle. Whether you are paid or not: know your worth. And in all things, strive to remember to pay as much attention to the small and meaningful moments which make the work worthwhile.

## JOB LOSS

There's no sugarcoating it, losing your job (or promotion or the job you thought you had in the bag) sucks. Whether you saw it coming or it came out of the blue, unless you intentionally put in your notice, job loss is a time of grief and uncertainty. If you have your wits about you, grab your favorite mug from the break room, negotiate severance, trade contact information with key people, collect documentation of wrongful termination (if applicable), and leave with your head held high. Now is not the time to stick it to "them", let karma take care of that. Your focus is now on *you.*

Which is all well and good, you're thinking, but how will you get by financially? Who among your former coworkers or regular customers will you miss horribly? It's normal to grieve this loss, but if I can humbly suggest: do so with the speed and intensity of a messy romantic breakup. Trust that whatever you thought you had, you are better off without them, and they will regret this decision, but that ship has sailed. Speed-grieve that loss and process your emotions as quickly as you can, because your former employer? They are fiiiiiiiine.

When you've cried the tears and powered through the intense workouts and eaten the junk food, take a shower, eat some nutritious something and make a plan. Sit down with a good friend and plot your next moves. Tell everyone you know that you are looking for an opportunity and ask if they know someone you might chat with in that area. Yes, search for listings and send in the applications and contact the recruiters as appropriate, but while resumes are run through and scanned by some computer somewhere, *humans* ultimately employ other *humans*. Cut out that middle bit as much as possible and connect with other humans. In the end, they know the way around their own bureaucracy. Ideally, you want someone on the inside pulling your application through the system as much as you are pushing from the outside. This process is ridiculously and painfully slow, though, so don't put off having honest conversations with loved ones about where you are financially and what that might mean. If it means taking on extra side work or cutting expenses or altering living situations, it's better to face those things head on and with honesty. You'll get through this as long as you face forward. Looking back doesn't serve you.

Now for your pep talk: Your former job loss? That awful day? That pain-filled experience? It was the only way Future You could move to that next, better place. Your job may have defined your days, your schedule, even your years for a while, but it doesn't and never did define *you*. You are so much more than that one thing you did for a while however much it consumed your time and attention. Now is the time for your next phase. You have learned so much since that first day on the job. You've evolved and grown. You bring maturity and experience to this next job you didn't have when you started your last one. And like a romantic breakup, you now know more precisely what you want and what you don't and are better able to articulate that. Who knows, perhaps the person you need to articulate that to is yourself, future entrepreneur.

In the physical sciences there is the oft-quoted phrase: inertia is a powerful force. An object at rest tests to stay at rest. But an object in motion? It will keep moving.

So, keep rolling, my friend. Keep rolling! Let this loss propel you forward, unburdened by the weight of what was. Think of the possibilities!

## RETIREMENT

Yes, think of the possibilities. That's the exact same advice I give to my friends looking toward retirement. For many, it feels like a vast open field of nothingness. It is a pasture where we are expected to meander around and selfishly but unproblematically entertain ourselves, grazing until we die.

Pretty depressing, that image, isn't it?

Let's reframe things, shall we?

Let's rename Retirement as our Next Phase. Those days working for others, working to put food on the table and a roof over our heads? If we are lucky, they are behind us. Or, at least, we hopefully don't have to work forty hours plus a week for basic necessities. In our Next Phase, we set our own schedule, immerse ourselves in those activities and pursuits we didn't have time for before. In this Next Phase, we *get to do* things we've put off like travel, or classes, or hobbies. More importantly, we get to *give back* in the form of volunteer work, mentoring, and community service that can take the form of running for local elected positions to working in any number of programs for youth, to community gardens, to online communities.

With all the experience and confidence we've gained from a lifetime of problem-solving, we can imagine and launch our own flavor of giving back, open a small business that suits our hours and interests, or go back to school to finish a degree or gain certification, because I'm here to tell you: this is it. This is your life.

This is your next phase to shape however you are able. But if you go into it thinking "I only have 10 or 15 good years left" I want you to think back at your life, tell me what you accomplished in any 10-15-year period and then ask yourself, what could I still do even if I were half as productive? One quarter?

More importantly, what if your next phase isn't only about you, but about the community of like-minded individuals you bring together? What can you accomplish? What shared joy can you experience?

It is well-known that those who are socially active as they age live longer, are healthier, and are more content. I don't know about you, but I would rather die half-way through attaining a big goal I was pursuing than to twiddle my thumbs for years waiting for the inevitable.

# PART 13

# SOCIAL MEDIA

# Chapter 20

## LIFE IN THE DIGITAL AGE

### HOW THE WORLD SEES US

I inhabit a unique generation which spans the before and after of the internet. It's an interesting perspective, and while I feel slower on the uptake sometimes, I recognize that life in the digital age is hard.

We are bombarded with information, misinformation, and disinformation (and the requirement to understand the differences therein) at a speed and volume we couldn't comprehend if we hadn't experienced it. We are both expected to know things about how to navigate ever-changing social spheres, but also to maintain our privacy and that of others.

The youth who have never experienced life without a screen haven't known what it's like to wait for news, what a sense of calm it is to not be privy to the trials and tribulations of *n*-billion souls at any given moment, and have only ever existed in a time where they've felt they had to market themselves to the world without having a finished product.

We all know, though, that the internet is the space we often meet others first, including romantic connections and business contacts, so how the world sees us online is important. It is also rife with pitfalls.

It's easy to fall into the trap of crafting an image that doesn't exist in real life, only to be found out to be a player, a poser, or some other negative characterization when some long-forgotten social media post or photograph rears its ugly head. The key to surviving this fraught landscape is as easy as telling the truth. Authenticity is the key to navigating the digital age, because the thing about the internet is that it is full of people looking for reality and others pretending to be something they are not.

So, show up as your true self. If that true self has unpleasant bits? Work on fixing those before revealing them to the world, because the internet never forgets.

You can have a schtick, a vlog, a channel, or a brand that viewers relate to and connect with. It may well be a facet of your true personality, but never forget that we all still exist in the physical plane and will inevitably cross paths and when that happens? Our goal is that that meeting will be seamless and a "so nice to finally meet you in person" moment and not a "you're not what I was expecting" moment.

First impressions matter, but it's the in-person impression that matters most.

## MANAGING OUR SOCIAL MEDIA PRESENCE

Back in my college days, my roommate took a photo of me in the dorm bathroom as I had face cleanser all over my face. She laughed and ran off. I was annoyed. I hadn't consented to that photo, and it wasn't an image I was keen on having widely distributed.

But she took it with an actual film camera. It may well have not come out well and certainly never existed on the internet.

Today, we are photographed and our image transmitted to platforms of thousands or millions of viewers in less time that it would have taken for that dorm bathroom door to swing shut. And that image we may want widely distributed can do real damage to our self-esteem, our reputation, and our future job and romantic prospects. Managing our social media presence matters.

Sure, there are services we can engage that will work to scrub our social media history and anyone running for office or going on a reality dating show should probably engage one, but I'm here to say it is also fair to ask those who are taking a picture to allow us to control what happens with that image. We can ask to see a photo before it's posted anywhere, tell them who may have access to it, ask to be cropped from it, or have them delete any images with us in them.

If we are taking photos of an event, particularly a public one, it is important to ask permission of strangers or blur their faces before posting online. If we are taking photos of a party or celebration, only include those at the party or event in the distribution list and ask others, out of courtesy, not to share outside the group.

We never know who out there is having issues with body dysmorphia, who has a stalker they are trying to avoid, or who may have other reasons for wanting to control where and when their image is tagged and disseminated.

It's hard when we want to share, but there are risks associated with posting pictures of young children or your beautiful daughter in that these posts can be used in AI manipulation or may attract unwanted attention. It is best to print them in photo books, post on our refrigerators or in frames, or send them with our annual holiday emails.

If a compromising photo of a minor is shared by a peer, it is legal and advisable to contact the platform it was shared on to take it down. I have privately requested a friend take down a photo of me that had me feeling less than positive about myself, because I would like to retain control of how my likeness is shared in this world, and true friends don't want us to feel badly about ourselves.

## UNDOING WRONGS THAT LAST FOREVER

Perhaps, though, the thing that is on the internet is something that isn't a question about vanity but speaks to a time when we were not our best self. Perhaps we posted or shared something ugly, cruel, insensitive or simply unenlightened. If we can, we can delete the post. That's a first step, but it existed and others saw it. Maybe they took screenshots.

If so, a public apology is in order. Own the mistake. Show how we've grown. Vow to do better.

The reality is, no one will reach adulthood without some digital missteps. It is how we move on from that mistake, how we acknowledge it, grow from it, and the authenticity and humanity we exhibit moving forward that matters.

## CONTROLLING OUR CONSUMPTION—TOUCH GROUND

The pace at which news and information comes at us in a digital world is not normal or sustainable. We have all experienced digital overwhelm or the feeling that if we look away for a brief time something cataclysmic will happen unless we're monitoring everything all the time all at once.

I'm stressed just reading that sentence.

I highly recommend intentionally putting our digital connectivity on mute on a regular basis in favor of sitting in nature, touching ground as they say, or engaging in in-person interactions. That vacation in that area with spotty cell service? Golden. Game night at home with the kids or friends? Perfection. Plan to have someone over for a shared meal or afternoon snacks. Go for a walk or hike or museum tour with a friend. Read a book—a physical one—while they still exist. Sit in a sunny window and pet a dog or cat or ferret. Garden. Do all the things that existed and made life meaningful before anyone knew of such a thing as the internet. Our digital devices are tools, but are never a substitute for other humans or enjoying our beautiful planet.

PART 14

# HOW TO BE HAPPY

# Chapter 21

## CHOOSING HAPPINESS

I know, there's horrible stuff happening in the world. But the truth is, *there always is.* At any moment that I might be capable of reaching for joy, another human somewhere in this world is in the depths of despair. Would they want me, in solidarity, to reject my joy? Would I want them to reject their joy if mine weren't immediately within reach?

I've known heartache and despair and soul-crushing grief, so when I tell you that I'm gonna grab joy with both hands and my teeth when it's in reach? *I am.*

### OUR "REALITY" IS AN ALGORITHM

We've all experienced it. We see some ad or suggested content, click on it, and then suddenly our feed is nothing but corgis, crochet projects, and cast-iron cooking recipes. (Me. That's my feed.)

For me, this is joyful. The next thing I know my feed has branched out into heartwarming golden retrievers frolicking amongst their stuffies, nature photos of Scotland, and videos of people dancing. All good!

It's clear that the more I turn my focus toward things that I enjoy, the more my personal algorithm sends those things my way. This is true both online and in real life.

It works in reverse, too, though. Click on one pimple popping video and you'll know what I mean. LOL In the past, as the world <waves vaguely> and those in my sphere felt more threatening, the content I saw and my resultant mood was one of anxiety and dread. Even when I turned away from the screens and toward those around me, I'd trained my brain to focus on the negativity in the world and often that's what I saw.

The mild, everyday inconveniences I experienced—from clumsily dropping something to having to run back for something I'd forgotten—became proof that things weren't going my way. A stubbed toe would lead to running late to feeling rushed to spilling something because I was rushed… You know what I'm describing. We've all had one of those "woke up on the wrong side of the bed" sort of days, but if we stop, turn around, and tell ourselves to start over, we can short-circuit this trajectory.

So why, when there are communities literally on fire am I so calm? How have I managed to retain that calm for weeks despite so much uncertainty and so much threatening rhetoric?

Am I a Pollyanna? Delusional? Engaging in toxic positivity? Disassociating?

Hopefully, none of those things. It feels more that I've come to see that I have the power to shape my perception, and my perception, to a large degree, shapes how I experience my reality. Like the main character in Ella Enchanted (Fabulous movie. Go enjoy it if you haven't seen it). She is told she's cursed to be obedient and then is told to do horrible things. It is not until she realizes that the power to change lies within that she can break free of the curse. She declares, "I will no longer be obedient." And so, it is true. I know; it's fiction, but there's a truth in it.

A while back, as I saw many around me fretting about what might happen in the future, I said to myself: I will no longer be fearful. I will allow myself to observe others behaving badly or acting out without it changing my perception of the goodness still present in the world at large. I will not "click on" the negativity. This is not to say that I intend to ignore the horrors in the world. I still make efforts to do my part when I feel I can make a positive difference.

There will always be toxic or alarming events in the world, but I can *choose* what I focus on. I can choose the corgis and travel vlogs and community building, and in so doing, I can shape my immediate reality.

Does such an approach negate the fraught lived experience of others? Absolutely not. I've lived through "fraught" times. We will likely face more of them as a collective. But what better serves us when the battle comes to our door? Does it serve us to have exhausted ourselves mentally, to have accepted the "curse" as truth? Or, are we better served to shore ourselves up with the joy that is possible and available in our individual lives so that we know what we are "fighting" for if and when we are confronted?

On any given day there may be events which threaten to steal our agency and peace, I encourage each of us to focus on training our personal algorithms in life and online to bring to us that which bring our lives meaning, stability, and groundedness.

Seek out your inner knowing, your own agency, so that you aren't so easily yanked around by the manipulations of others. Be prepared to deflect those who try to tell you you can't feel your joy.

Find your center. Find your breath. Claim your joy.

## WHAT TOXIC POSITIVITY IS AND ISN'T

If you recoil when you read that heading, give me a minute. We have all heard of toxic positivity, the whole "be happy" directive that feels as if it's attempting to nullify our trauma, daily hardships, and real-world struggles by telling us to get over it and that our grief, pain, and anxiety are simply states of mind. The previous paragraphs may reinforce that belief. I have a different take on this, though.

I also reject a toxic positivity which assumes that there is no dark side of life if we simply don't acknowledge it. Optimism, for me, also falls into the camp of a perspective which assumes that good things will happen versus assuming that things will happen—both good *and* bad—and that our response is both a choice and a way to cope.

When I "Choose Happy" I am acknowledging that something has made me feel sad, pained, lonely, disillusioned, fearful, what-have-you-negative-emotion. My response to that event or feeling, though, *is* within my control. Even the most awful occurrence can, after reflection or with distance, be framed with gratitude. Even if I can't immediately be thrilled and laughing that my husband was hospitalized with a life-threatening infection (true story) and I was exhausted from running up the stairs to care for him then down the stairs to care for my teen recovering from knee surgery, in those days I distinctly remember laughing at the absurdity of my situation. I remember saying to myself, "This is *great* exercise," while recognizing it was not a choice I'd made to dash up and down our staircase countless times day and night.

But, I had the choice to joke about it to myself. I indulged in taking a break to hug the cat whose fur was soft, purrs were soothing, and who still looked at me for food on a schedule despite my clear busyness. When friends would swing by with prepared meals that both filled my nutritional needs but were sensitive to the vegetarian preferences of my daughter, I felt loved and grateful and not once did I lament that we were the charity case others were taking pity on. When I was my most exhausted, I allowed myself to sob on a friend's shoulder, and then I'd crack a joke and we would laugh through our tears, because as bad as it was—and it was bad, friends—I was *living through it* and I knew I'd find my way back to more stable ground eventually. So, I allowed myself to choose happy. I didn't force it. I didn't demand it of myself or others, and I didn't pretend the worry, heartache, and pain I was feeling didn't exist. I simply allowed the laughter, the absurdity, the irony, the are-you-effing-kidding-me messy and human reality of it all to bubble up, take some of the awfulness off my shoulders and float away.

When I choose happy or choose joy, I am recognizing that to *remain* in a space of grief or worry is often a choice we make. Perhaps we feel we don't have the energy to find humor in a situation. Perhaps we feel that laughing or finding something to smile about takes away from the gravity of the moment or implies we don't feel sad or awful enough to warrant pity or help.

Yes, for many it is truly a struggle to lift up out of despair. I have been there, too.

Back when I was a young mother, I became pregnant with my second child. I was thrilled. Unfortunately, at twelve weeks along, I miscarried. A month later I was hospitalized with sepsis. After four days, I was sent home, weak, mentally and physically depleted, but alive.

The infection had inflamed the tissues in my abdomen, and I hadn't felt a pain that intense since birthing my son. It was excruciating to move. I remember laying on the living room couch as my husband hurried to the pharmacy for pain meds with our two-year-old. I was alone.

I was alone. Exhausted. Scared. In pain.

I began to cry, silent tears sliding down my cheeks, because I couldn't do *this* anymore. Merely existing felt overwhelming. I couldn't do it alone. I was our family's sole breadwinner, a mother, a wife, and I felt so badly battered and broken I couldn't see how I could make my way back to strong and functional and whole again.

I cried and then spoke aloud. "I can't do this. I can't do this alone. I need help."

*I can't do this alone.*

My mistake and the reason I struggled is because I felt I had to fight the battle alone. In the hospital the nurse had admonished me when she found me curled into a fetal position of pain, tears streaming down my face. She said, "We can get you pain meds. You should have said something." (By the way, she was wonderful and comforting and competent and *right*. I should have said something.)

I didn't have to do it alone. I could ask for help.

On that cold autumn day, something shifted when I finally asked God, the universe, creation, for help. The moment I gave up the feeling that I was alone in solving all that was wrong, I wasn't alone anymore. As soon as I admitted I needed help, help arrived.

My husband returned, pain meds and comfort foods in hand. My son was there, smiling his toddler smile. My mother came to help so that my son and husband had support, too. We were all battling a challenging time but chose to cling to one another.

In the background, as our small family leaned in for support, we had yet more assistance. The man who had been working to upgrade our septic system finished the job while I was still in the hospital then barely charged for materials knowing we had hospital bills to cover.

In my grief and then illness I had been siloing myself, and the more I rejoined the community of family, friends, and caregivers, the more I recognized they had been there all along. It was as if they had their hands outstretched to reach me and *us* and we had only to accept the outstretched hands of assistance to form the circle.

I recovered quickly, returned to work, and within two months my husband was offered a position unsolicited in his prior field of work. We decided it was the right choice for our family for us to switch roles. He began his new job in February. In March I found out I was pregnant again. Our daughter was born the following December.

As I look back upon the times in my life when I have felt beaten down, defeated, or grief-stricken, I also see the moment that choosing the outstretched hands of community—however that is defined—is the moment I chose joy. It was in those moments where I made the choice to seek out help that I realized it was there waiting for me to see it, interact with it, feel it supporting me in the many ways I needed support.

I have felt chronic pain from a pinched nerve in my neck. I spent several years with daily pain that would radiate to my temple. I tried chiropractor treatments, muscle relaxants, stretches. Ice. Heat. An endless stream of acetaminophen and ibuprofen. Those who have read this far are probably thinking, yeah, you asked for help and didn't feel better.

Eventually, I went to a skilled osteopath who was able to treat me and, finally, after another six months of care, I found lasting relief.

Which is my way of admitting that, yes, there *are* times we reach for that hand and all it can provide is comfort and the knowledge that we do not have to be alone in our struggle.

Sometimes there is no relief to be had. Sometimes the joy to be found is in the connections with others that say "we see you struggling and you are not alone." And that? That has to be where we find our joy. That has to be where we find our gratitude.

## HOW HOPE AND HAPPINESS INTERSECT

---

*Hope is believing in the possibility of good outcomes despite the odds.*
*Faith is trusting there is a way there even when we can't see it.*

---

Over time I've shared social media posts where I've encouraged others to find ways to be grateful, to have faith, to feel joy when and where they can. Most have been well received, but I'd be lying if I claimed universal approval. Over the months, I've also had my share of comments accusing me of both being out-of-touch with the moment and spreading toxic positivity.

Ouch.

Naturally, when I read such comments, I feel both defensive (which, BTW, I've found is an excellent moment to pause, reflect, and think hard about why I'm feeling that way) and misunderstood. I've sat with these thoughts, mulling over both the comments and my own triggers, because the very last thing I want to do is gaslight others about their own reality and deny their valid feelings.

But the misunderstood part? That I have come to some clarity on. And this is it:

Optimism is believing all and only good things are coming. (This is where toxic positivity comes from.)

Pessimism is believing all and only bad things will happen. (This is sometimes the space commenters are pushing back from.)

Realism understands that both good *and* bad things happen to all people.

*Hope* is accepting the reality of the present moment yet holding space for even the slim possibility of something wonderful to come.

Hope is faith that in a universe where both good and bad things happen that the possibility always exists for something good.

I am a hopeful, hope-filled realist.

In any moment where all is changing and so many are suffering, I hold fast to the possibility that anything could happen—including some very amazing and wonderful things. And I choose, for my sanity and peace of mind, to focus on that possibility however much my current reality allows me to.

## RIGHTEOUS ANGER

---

*Hope believes the inclusive and loving future we long for is possible.*
*Faith is the vehicle we ride to our destination.*
*Righteous outrage is the fuel.*

---

It might seem an odd place to plunk a section on anger, here in the section on how to be happy, but bear with me, because it feels the perfect place to acknowledge that sometimes? Yeah. Happiness is *not* what we're feeling, and no amount of reframing our perspective, gratitude practice, or glimmer of hope will change that. I'm not here to invalidate anyone's feelings or to claim that I, somehow, am immune to feelings of anger, as my friends who I vent to on our many long walks can attest.

We all feel it, those of us living and breathing in this world as humans, so what *is* anger and how do we deal with this fiery emotion?

It's one thing to feel annoyed, frustrated, or betrayed when we are directly impacted by events, words, or situations that harm or impede us. Most of us are familiar with this emotion and can navigate this type of anger more readily. We can think of solutions, communicate our desire for amends, or otherwise diffuse the heat of the moment. Actions to be taken are usually immediately apparent.

But injustice triggers something slightly different in us. Our righteous outrage rises up when we feel someone doesn't value something we hold dear—whether that's human life, human rights, our world, or social mores. It often sparks feelings of helplessness and victimization when we are harmed or an empathetic anger on behalf of others. Righteous outrage doesn't arise from every offense; it is a response to someone crossing a boundary we hold sacred.

Sometimes the outrages of the world come so fast and furious we don't know how to respond. We're so overwhelmed with the enormity of our feelings, the injustices, or the scale of the offenses that we don't know what the next best action should be.

As I write this, humanity is experiencing a great deal of political chaos and humanitarian crises. Governments are acting out against their people and neighboring lands. Individuals and groups are being targeted, kidnapped and trafficked. Corruption is rampant and blatant. Gaslighting is at an all-time high.

I have found myself paying less attention to the 24/7 news streams, not because I don't care and want to keep myself in an ignorant bubble, but because it is far too easy to allow the day-to-day outrage-du-jour to hijack my thoughts and lead me down a spiral of overwhelm and paralysis. It is much better for me to check in periodically, to take the pulse of things, and then pull away so that I can better think through the best path forward from a place of relative calm.

Mind you, I recognize the importance of righteous outrage in motivating me (and others) to take action—to stand up for the vulnerable among us. But far too often I've felt that that outrage had no immediate outlet. That's when it becomes dangerous. It either turns inward—churning into hate—or outward in pessimism, harmful stereotyping, and other negativity that threatens to harden me and make me less able to hear the nuggets of truth from unwelcome places.

So, I gently ask you, should you be feeling that familiar fire in your belly:

---

*Is your anger paralyzing you, poisoning you, or propelling you forward toward positive change?*

---

Your answer is a guide to how you should respond.

Our anger is our passion ignited, our deepest desire for *change*. We must be careful it doesn't set us or our world on fire. Instead, we must *use it* to light the way. To fuel justice activism and progress. To stand guard as the vulnerable find and use their voices. To urge others to stand up and stand firm against those who would harm them, humanity, wildlife, or our natural world.

---

*Be sure your anger serves you, never the other way around.*

---

PART 15

# THE GIFT OF GRATITUDE

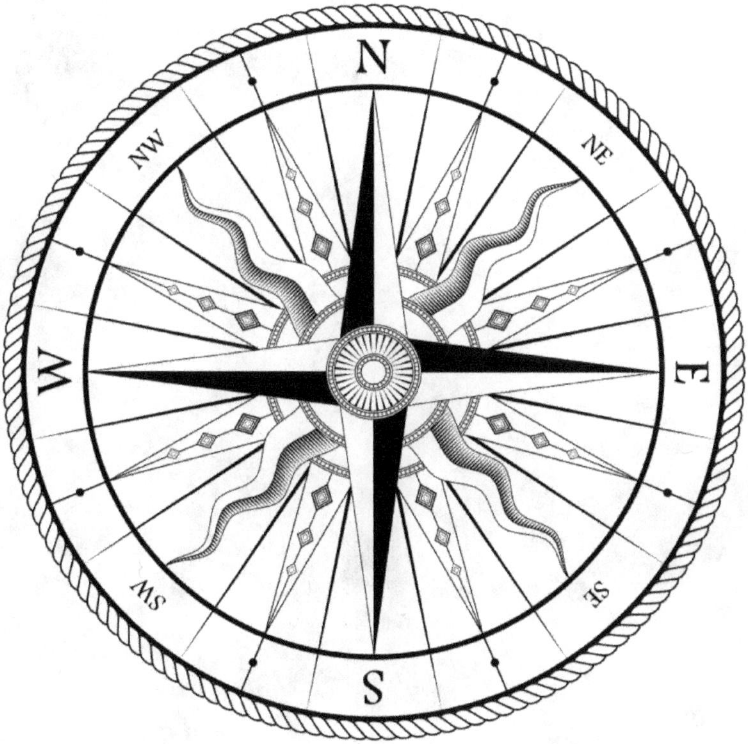

# Chapter 22

## GRATITUDE & CELEBRATION

### A GRATEFUL LIFE – MY MOTHER

My mother was widowed at the age of 63.

She retired at 70.

She was diagnosed with an incurable degenerative muscular disease not long after.

She was 85 when she died.

While all these facts are true, she will be remembered as being one of the most joyful and gratitude-filled humans I and many of her acquaintance have ever met.

When my father passed, she spoke of how grateful she was to have all four of her children living nearby to help out. She was in the room when my son was born just three short months after being widowed and commented that had Dad still been with us, she would have been home caring for him and missed seeing her youngest grandson being born. She taught her grandchildren how to drive and came for sleepover babysitting for my kids bringing the latest movies to share with them.

When my children were young, she drove to our house every week to do arts and crafts and science experiments with them and came to the science museums with her cane and a smile that said go and explore and we will catch up when I get there.

As her balance grew less certain she began to use a walker especially on uneven terrain.

One day the kids wanted to play badminton, something they remembered doing with their grandmother in earlier years. I insisted it wasn't a good day for it, but Mom? She had other plans.

She made her way out and stood in the middle of our yard, one hand on her walker, the other holding a racket. From there she joyfully played badminton with her grandkids for a solid half hour.

I will never forget the example she showed all of us that day. She could have begged off or asked for sympathy, but she chose life and when she came in professed gratitude for such a beautiful afternoon then asked for lemonade.

In the coming years she would eventually be confined to a wheelchair and need assistance with even the most basic of daily activities. We would visit and adapted her favorite word games so we all could have fun.

Even when she had to find a friend who was able to manipulate jigsaw puzzle pieces for her, she cheerfully pointed toward the piece she'd found and tell them where it went.

Every holiday season she bought chocolates for the staff and made sure to tell every person she came across to go to the third floor nurse's station to get their treat.

After she passed, we received a card of condolence signed by all the staff speaking of how much they missed her and her positive attitude, including the kitchen and janitorial staff.

She expressed gratitude for every small gift and in so doing spent some of the most challenging years of her life feeling blessed.

## CELEBRATION: GRATITUDE IN ACTION

---

*Celebration is gratitude in action.*

---

There is likely never going to be a moment in our adult lives when we are completely free of stress, worry, grief, or distractions. We will nearly always feel that we don't have enough time or the mental bandwidth to be present for each other, and all I have to say is: make the time. Make the time as best you can.

My father was diagnosed with ALS in the spring of 1998. That summer would mark my parents' 42nd wedding anniversary. I was determined to celebrate this marriage and these people while we could, so I invited the whole family: my siblings, their spouses and partners and all the nieces and nephews to the first ever Family Day.

It was an elaborate day filled with silly games.

We held a relay race in which we navigated a course filled with activities like, "dance from the garage to the camper," and then a section of the course where you put on a blindfold, reached into a paper bag, put on three random items, then made a mad dash to the finish line using your teammates' voices to guide you.

I will never forget the image of my father, wearing a scarf, a sideways apron, and a single oven mitt as he—a typically quiet and introverted man—laughed his way toward the unseen finish line.

We completed the afternoon with a "Newlywed Game" where my parents answered questions about each other and their lives and "won" a fabulous all-expense paid trip to their back yard.

After the games, we stuffed ourselves with our favorite summer potluck munchies then collapsed in various spots in my parents' big sprawling downstairs. Despite the cloud of my father's diagnosis, we rejoiced in what we still had together.

Dad passed the following April. In July I had my son. Life was upside-down, but we all decided it would be too sad to let August—my parents' anniversary month—go by without a family gathering, so the Second Annual Family Day was planned.

Over the years, as other holidays pulled us in divergent directions, Family Day was for celebrating *us*. We took joy in creating ever more elaborate themes, game ideas, and menus.

We had the Wild West Family Day where we pitted "boys" against "girls" with a hidden stash of valuables high in a tree. The girls' team found the prize early in the game and unbeknownst to me, the game creator, replaced it with fistfuls of pine cones and leaves, stashing the real treasure elsewhere. It was a heist no one predicted and led to much friendly ribbing.

There was Treasure Island Family Day with the kiddie pool filled with sand and hidden clues and another kiddie pool where you had to "blow" your ship to the other side before continuing on your journey.

We had the Muppets Murder Mystery, Murder on the Orient Express (complete with assigned characters and costumes) in which we were mailed "tickets" in invitation, Tropical Paradise with volcano-blazoned t-shirts, and more.

Even after my mother, a decade later, resided in a nursing home, my siblings and I worked with her to organize a family day gathering in the home's outdoor patio area. The theme? Summer Fun, of course.

After Mom passed, it was obvious how we would celebrate her life. We gathered first at the gravesite for our solemn prayers and remembrances, and a recorded piano composition from my eldest. Then we said our final goodbyes on that sunny hillside, and drove to my sister's home for games and potluck food as Mom would have so thoroughly enjoyed.

Family Day was something we all made time for, took time off for, and prepared for because it mattered. The games, the menu, even the date changed from year to year, but the important bit was always the gathering.

It was not perfect. The games were made up and sometimes didn't go as planned. I'm here to tell you, though, that none of that ever mattered.

It's the community and connections in our lives that are worth celebrating, and the people who matter won't care about any imperfect details and will be thrilled to be a part of our celebrations.

It will come as no surprise to you, that my own nuclear family has hosted many a gathering over the years. We've done winter wonderland parties for our daughter's December birthday, Fancy Dress parties where friends came in thrift-store prom gowns, summertime birthday sleepovers with adventurous parents, tents dotting our lawn, and a big, hearty breakfast in the morning. We've had friends over for dinner both planned and spontaneous, baptism luncheons, graduation parties for multiple teens with lawn chairs and a giant sheet cake whose bright red flowers stained all our teeth. We have chosen to take every excuse to celebrate life with those we love and cherish and those memories are some of my most treasured in part because we made time for each other. We were intentional about saying: you matter, and because you matter, I am making time to celebrate life with you.

Don't let the busyness, stress, or financial strains of our everyday lives get in the way of gathering and being joyful. Where there is a will there is a way, and where there is family—whether by birth or by choice—there is every reason and opportunity to celebrate.

Play the games. Make the music. Eat the food.

In the end, when we look back at all of life, it's the moments we spend with others which stand out.

## ABUNDANCE VS. SCARCITY

If you've read this far, you will have picked up on an overarching theme, but I'm here to hammer it home, because it is *the* theme. We can choose to be happy, hopeful, and joy-filled if we turn our focus toward that which we are grateful for. The choice of "choosing joy" isn't about deciding to be magically happy, it's seeing the world as holding an abundance of blessings which can be found in the midst of the trials.

In the words of Inigo Montoya: "To sum up:"

---

*Despair and grief exist in a space of scarcity,*
*loss, and want.*
*Happiness is found in gratitude.*

---

Before you come at me with the pitchforks, I admit there are times that want, chaos, and scarcity are loudly demanding attention. When I was nursing two family members back to health on separate floors of the house and then the water heater sprang a leak? I'm pretty sure my first words weren't ones of gratitude.

It is for those choice moments when the world is spiraling out of control that I wrote this next section.

PART 16

# JUST EXHALE

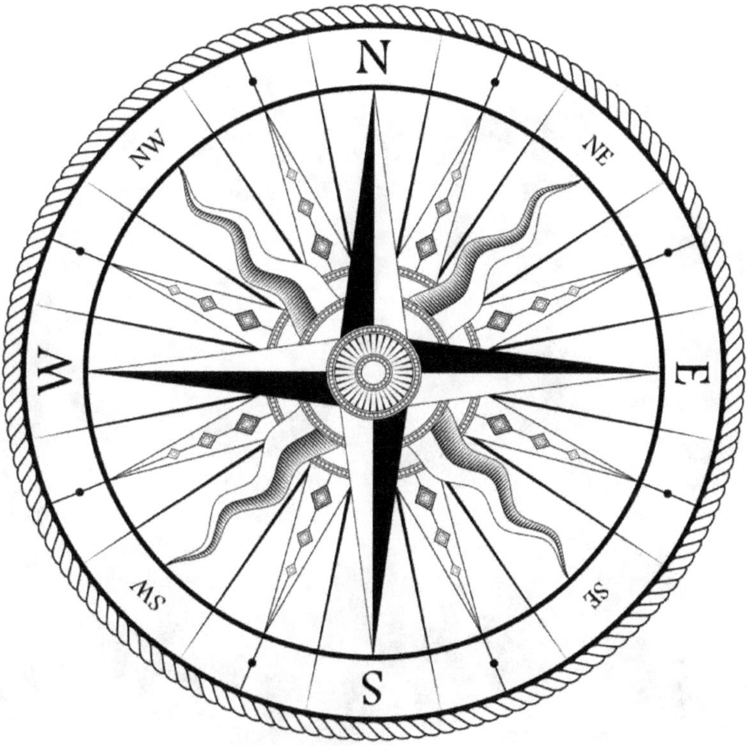

# Chapter 23

## FINDING CALM WHEN THE WORLD IS SPINNING

### MINDFULNESS, BREATH AWARENESS, AND MORE

I have been in the midst of the storm of life before. In those moments where we are so overwhelmed we struggle to breathe, our feet feel swept from beneath us, and we don't know where to focus, it's ridiculous to expect to feel gratitude or even make basic decisions. Perhaps we may feel disconnected from our body, reality, or that which keeps us centered and steady.

I have several strategies that have worked for me when I have sought to move from dysregulated and reactive to a more grounded, cerebral, and emotionally-regulated state of being,

The next time you find yourself swept away in the currents of life, perhaps you can try one of these strategies on for size. I hope it will help you feel less overwhelmed.

- **Feel your feet**. Go barefoot and place your feet flat on grass or the floor. Notice the sensation of the floor. Is it cold? Smooth? Do the blades of grass tickle? Feel the ground or floor pushing up against your soles. Wiggle each toe in turn. Now imagine you are planting your body above your feet, feeling your feet grow roots deep into the earth. Imagine that the earth is providing nourishment and energy back up through your feet, into your trunk, and you are now able to stretch your arms up, up to the sky like a living tree. Feeling your feet is an excellent grounding technique to return focus to your body when you are feeling lost in chaotic thought.

- **Describe your surroundings.** This strategy helps to return your focus to your immediate surroundings. Focus on anything in your immediate space. Now, describe what you see aloud or in your head. "I see a clock. It is white with black trim. It's small. It's on a table. The table is dark and has turned legs. I see a carpet. It is floral. Big flowers. Blue and white and some green." You get the idea. The more you describe the space you are in, the more senses you include in your noticing, the more you return your thoughts and attention to your surroundings.

- **Imagine a fan is on. Then turned off.** This is a quick strategy for bringing a space back into focus similar to the one above but rather than focusing on visual input the focus is on auditory inputs. Imagine that there is a loud fan running—that is your chaotic mind. Now, turn the fan off. What about your immediate surroundings comes to your attention? Name them in your mind or aloud. If what you notice is visual or a scent and not a sound, that's okay! It all works the same.

- **Be present in your body.** Take a hot or cold shower, dance, stretch, touch grass, cook nourishing food and eat it with intention, listen to instrumental music which uplifts your soul, or meditate. Do anything which asks you to be present in your body and mind. This can be helpful if we are feeling a persistent lack of groundedness or lack of focus. It can bring our emotional and physical state back to center and back to neutrality.

- **Be in the flow.** This strategy may work for redirecting thoughts that are moving in a negative direction particularly when we feel we are overwhelmed with empathy, negative energy, or the traumatizing experiences of others. Imagine yourself as an engine of transmutation. Be in the flow of experiencing the negative feelings, but imagine yourself then transmuting them through your empathy into the feeling of love, the image of light, the scent of mint or citrus, or whatever says "fresh" to your brain. You are allowed to momentarily feel those negative feelings on behalf of others, but not to hold onto them. It is your job to transmute them into love, light, or neutrality. This gives your brain a task to perform as opposed to a state to wallow in.

- **Connect your light.** This exercise works well for me when I'm feeling adrift, alone, or insignificant. Imagine you are a small light. Now imagine that your small light shines out of you and reveals someone you love or care about. See their illuminated face in your mind's eye. See their light ignite as yours touches them. Now imagine their light doing the same for another. Expand your perspective as the circles of connectedness grows wider until you are able to envision the glow of shared illuminance circling the world and shining back upon you. I especially enjoy this practice as I drift off to sleep.

## HOW TO BREATHE

Fun story: when I was in labor with our first-born, my husband was concerned I was hyperventilating. (I wasn't.) He insisted I focus on him and match my breaths to his. I tried, but it felt like I would pass out from lack of oxygen. He insisted. I ignored.

Somehow our baby was born.

Years later he enrolled as a participant in a respiratory research study, and we learned he has an abnormally slow respiration rate.

Who among us has found ourselves in the midst of crisis and had someone tell us (unhelpfully) to "just breathe"? We might ignore them, or we might hyper-fixate on our stressor, force some deep breaths, and return to hyper-fixating on our stressor, annoyed that "just breathing" didn't work. Or, we might attempt to control our breath, matching some numeric pattern of inhaling, exhaling, holding, alternating nose and mouth and suddenly our blood pressure is higher, our breath is not even cooperating, and we are more stressed than before.

This had been my prior experience with "breathing to be calm" when my husband was suddenly hospitalized and told an organ transplant was his best hope, our teen was undergoing bone-graft surgery after a year of unsuccessful and painful treatments, and my mom had recently passed. I was at the end of my emotional rope. I was barely surviving, swinging wildly between the logistics of each day's hospital runs and pet care and a thousand worries about estate planning, finances, and whether we had food to eat in the house.

It was in this space that a dear friend who served as our own lighthouse in this stormy period sat with me at my husband's bedside and said, "Let's focus on our breath."

*Let's focus on our breath.*

Bless her, she did not tell us to follow some complicated breathing pattern but shared with us a technique based on the teachings of Vietnamese monk and peace activist, Thich Nhat Hanh, and it changed everything for me.

In those moments where our minds are scattered and overwhelmed and we feel we are watching our lives unfold from an emotionally detached and safe distance, or so overwhelmed by the storm that the waves won't let us catch our breath, the most helpful thing to do is this:

***Observe your breath.***

Don't try to change it in any way. Just notice it happening. Turn your focus to the fact that you are inhaling and exhaling. If you find your mind straying, don't get angry with yourself, just focus again, perhaps tell yourself: "I am inhaling. I am exhaling." Watch your breath. Feel it filling your lungs and feel it emptying again, like gentle waves. Chances are good, you are, in fact, breathing. Just congratulate yourself on this act and be present with it.

You will begin to notice that as you observe your breath, *without even trying*, your breath will slow and become more regular. Continue to observe and feel how your breathing brings your focus back to *here* and *now.*

Focusing on your breathing brings your attention back to your physical body and away from your racing thoughts. If you were in fight or flight mode, feel how the attention to breathing relaxes your limbs. Feel the heaviness in your arms, your legs, your feet. If possible, wiggle your toes, feel the sensation of the pressure of the floor beneath your feet pressing up against your soles. Feel your groundedness.

In focusing on our breath—the most basic and automatic function of our bodies—we allow ourselves to come back to center. No decisions can be made, no actions can be taken, if we feel disconnected from our physical form and our minds are racing in every direction.

So, when someone tells you to breathe, take that as a reminder that if you hear those words, you already *are* breathing, and, instead, focus your attention on your breath to bring you to a place of calm and centeredness.

***Just Exhale.***

Thich Nhat Hanh's method is all well and good unless we find ourselves so dysregulated we can't focus on anything or we find the act of focusing in and of itself stressful. (I see you, my neuro-spicy friends.) For you, I have an alternative, action-based approach to try: *Just exhale.* Don't count, don't worry about your nose or mouth, simply blow out a long breath and completely empty your lungs. Wait. Now do it again. And again. That's it. Notice I'm not telling you to inhale, because you are already doing that. (Hooray, you!) I'm not telling you to focus, because you'll be doing that naturally. I'm asking you to engage in an action: exhale.

Exhale until your brain has oxygen again and you are feeling less frantic. Exhale all the stress and worry and thoughts clogging your brain. Blow it out. When you are back in your body, try some of the grounding techniques mentioned earlier. I'm not asking you to meditate, but I encourage you to hug someone. That physical contact? That pressure of a solid hug? That can do wonders for those who struggle with anxiety and racing thoughts. Connect to yourself, connect to the world around you, and connect with one another.

## FINDING OUR INNER PEACE

I want to take a moment to speak about those times we're not feeling so calm and peaceful. I try to work hard to transmute my anger into actionable, righteous outrage and not hate. But—*hoo boy!*—there is a lot of cruelty, disdain, and corruption in the world. I know that for a lot of those who engage in negative or manipulative behaviors, "flooding the zone" and overwhelming others into submission or inaction is the whole point.

But I refuse to let go of hope. Hope is believing a future we long for is possible. Without hope, the overwhelm wins. If hope is the destination, righteous outrage is the fuel.

This is why emotional regulation through breath work, grounding, and other strategies is so important. We must treat our joy and inner peace as expensive. Don't give those away for free!

PART 17

# CONCLUDING THOUGHTS

# Chapter 24

## LOVE REALLY IS THE ANSWER

There is a parable you may have heard about called *The Parable of the Long Spoons.* It illustrates how the circumstances we view as hellish or heavenly may remain identical except for how the people treat one another. The story can be summarized as follows:

After death, souls are sent to heaven and hell. In each location, the inhabitants are seated along either side of tables piled with food, but all they have for utensils are long spoons, too long to feed oneself. The situations are entirely identical.

In hell, the people cannot cooperate, and consequently starve. In heaven, the diners feed one another across the table and are sated and happy.

The story speaks to how community, cooperation, and love are all that separates heaven from hell.

Love really is the answer.

### LOVE WHEN IT IS HARD TO DO SO – ZOOM OUT

We know that love and love for others is the basis of the Golden Rule, codified in every major religious practice around the globe. Love yourself. Love your neighbor. Love even when it is hard to do so. Lead with love.

I'm not going to lie. Loving is sometimes very hard. Staring into the face of our bullies, abusers, or even those who simply aren't hearing us, can be emotionally challenging. When I am faced with those emotional triggers that make me want to lash out rather than lead with love, I tell myself to zoom out. Zoom out past my own feelings, past another's anger, apathy, and hurtful actions, zoom out to a space of being able to view the situation, the totality of it with emotional neutrality.

I might be far out in time or space by the time I reach that point, years perhaps, but from there I should be able to give all involved unconditional love.

You can love yourself enough to stand up for yourself and give yourself a voice, to find the courage to leave a situation that's harming you. You might be able to zoom out enough to see that this other person is speaking from a place of concern but also trauma. Or, maybe you can zoom out enough to see that their demons are theirs to conquer and that by allowing them to victimize you and not setting boundaries, you are denying them the opportunity for growth and healing.

With practice, zooming out teaches us how to respond with love rather than simply react. It brings us into a space of proactive control rather than allowing others to whipsaw us and our emotions. It brings us to that space of loving neutrality which helps keep the smaller frustrations of life in perspective and allows for a view of the horizon where hope resides. Win-win-win.

## LOVE YOURSELF THROUGH YOUR TRAUMA

I want to speak a moment about traumatic experiences, because chances are good you have lived through or might be living through them now. I won't tell you everything happens for a reason, because that's not up to me to decide and, honestly, I don't think it's as helpful as some would like to believe. I can say it about my own experiences, but it feels dismissive and invalidating of the real pain experienced in this life to have someone say it to another. What's the reason behind the loss of a child? Disease or war, famine, or abuse? It feels cruel for someone else to minimize or excuse the awful things that can happen in this life with a pat phrase.

But, I do wonder how we would feel if we imagined our soul *chose* these experiences in this life. You might think of all the horrific things you've been through and wonder why you'd ever choose them, that that's a ridiculous concept and you reject it out of hand. Fair enough. But what if you chose experiences of bullying or abuse to learn how to stand up for yourself, to demand respect, to use your voice not just for yourself but to advocate for the rights and humanity of others? What if you used your ability to find the good in dark circumstances, to remain hopeful despite being knocked down, to choose grief to prove to yourself and others that joy can and does exist after despair? What if your soul chose unspeakable challenges to see if you would succumb to hatred or find and rejoice in the power of love and the grace of acceptance?

What if you simply need to love yourself first to see others as lovable?

I'm not going to tell you that everything happens for a reason, because that's for you to decide and discover for yourself. But that journey of discovery? It may well be the "reason" you're searching for.

## WHAT IT MEANS TO HOLD THE LIGHT

In the story I told about my friend and I and our accumulating mutual debt, what made our approach work is that we both see the world from a place of abundance. We assume there is enough for all so long as we share what we have. This can be hard for those who have always felt resource-deprived.

What I've observed is that this sense of scarcity vs. abundance tends to slop over from views of money, having or have-notting, to a whole worldview where all resources are scarce including time and love. If one sibling is receiving attention, there is less for me. If one person is healthy, I must be sick. If another has good fortune, I'm sure to be down on my luck.

A scarcity mindset tells us that everything can be measured on a scale and if the thing I want in my life is observed to be in the possession of someone else, I must be lacking.

But there's another worldview I invite you to try on. What if, every time we see someone else experience something, we choose to add it to our metaphorical treasure trove? We see them experiencing something wonderful and so now we know that that wonderful thing exists. Soon, we have amassed a hoard of good things to dream about and marvel over: goodwill, abundant resources, things to eat, safe spaces to be.

Now, imagine we come across someone who is lacking something. We decide to share from our bounty. They are happy because we erased their lack. We look back at our treasure trove and realize we don't even notice anything missing.

This is how I feel when I go through my life.

I feel like every time I've seen something that another has acquired—friendships, talents, community—and I invite those treasures into my own life, they come hand-in-hand with practical and concrete benefits of food, shelter, and the like. The more I treat others as I would have them treat me, the more we are there for one another with the metaphorical checkbook from which to bail each other out when we find ours not at hand. The more we are there with a job offer out of the blue or a bargain-priced car when it's needed most, the more we are simply and efficiently reallocating the abundance of this existence.

A scarcity or zero-sum mindset robs us of our peace and traps us in a state of want and deprivation. It also pits us against one another and breeds jealousy and ill will.

But an abundance mindset? It brings everything we need into our lives. Based in gratitude and generosity, it changes everything.

The first step is to heal the wounds that we have. Come to terms with incorporating any losses we've experienced or accepting any grief we may carry. When we are whole and at peace, we can move forward in partnering with others, pursuing our passions, exploring our unique gifts, and sharing them with the world.

If we believe or act as if our individual light is the only way to navigate a dark and scary existence, we become desperate to protect it. What if there's a wind? What if I fall? What if I run out of fuel?

What if, though, we *all* stayed in connected community and shared our light wherever we find ourselves and with whomever might need it? Then, if someone amongst us falters, they have our collective light to see the way forward. They have our lights from which to reignite their own.

Love *is* the answer regardless of the question.

# Chapter 25

## FINAL WORDS

---

*Love is not transactional. It does not score-keep.*

*In times of conflict, love seeks connection, not a side.*

*Unconditional love is just that—love without conditions. It is the love that delights in human existence.*

---

Some readers may see in the cover of this book the colors of the bi pride flag. I didn't until it was pointed out, but I'm not mad about it. In fact, I'm secretly delighted at the way I have been guided along the path of bringing this book into being.

I've been toying with this book for years, wondering if it was mine to write. Wondering if I was up to the task. Wondering if I would do it justice.

As part of my creative process, I often create a mock-up of the cover art which serves as inspiration and motivation as I write. I poured over countless images in my search for one that spoke to me, and the primary image you see of the lighthouse and background colors stood out to me. I kept coming back to it.

As most creatives will tell you, their art is a small amount of ego and a greater proportion of divine inspiration—the "flow" or "muse" if you will. So, while my choice wasn't consciously intentional, I feel it was divinely guided, and so I happily kept my original choice, because a cover which celebrates living authentically for a book about loving yourself and the world without judgment makes perfect sense to me.

As I write this final chapter I see clearly: this book is as much one of rebellion as one of acceptance. It is a rebellion against division, human-made hierarchies, and harm disguised as "the way things are" or "the way things have always been." It is a rebellion against the status quo, isolationist beliefs, scarcity mindset, othering, and ego-centric living.

It is a book about radical love. Acceptance. *Joy.*

It is less about me telling you what you should do, and more what I hope you open yourself to the possibility of.

We have one life in this human meat-suit—this specific one if we believe in reincarnation. One chance to explore this world from this particular vantage-point—to smell the scents, taste the flavors, see the vistas, and feel the emotions unique to *us* and our experience.

The truth is, even though this is a book of advice, observations, and experiential anecdotes, I don't have all the answers and even if I did, do you really want them? Half the delight of this life we're living is the surprise of what's around the corner. But I've had my share of unwelcome surprises, rough patches and soul-crushing despair, too, so I also appreciate the value of a heads-up.

*Part 17: Concluding Thoughts.*

If I could give my younger self anything it would be this book. Having these insights would have helped me not so much avoid the rough times but see beyond them to the miracles that awaited me on the other side.

It would have helped me see the blessing in losing my father while pregnant with my first-born, because it meant my mother would be present to welcome her newest grandchild. It would give me the comfort that despite his not being physically here, he had given me so much, from his sense of humor to his life lessons, that I feel his love to this day.

This book would have provided reassurance that the challenging days of raising a neurodivergent kiddo would work out and to just be in the moment however overwhelming and messy it might seem at the time. It would have helped me see my child's nonconformity as the superpower it has come to be and to have let myself let go of the worry that only served to keep me up at night.

This book would have saved me years of questioning myself and my identity as a compassionate person so that I could enact healthy boundaries with those who did not have my best interests at heart.

This book would have shown me that, in the end, I don't need a book. All I really need is to remember that I am loved. And there is always enough love to go around. That loving connection is the key to so many things.

So, heal your wounds. Chase your passions. Fill your well with so much love that it spills over sloppily everywhere you go.

Let your love be like glitter that leaves a trail for others to follow and reminds them to live sparkly, authentic lives—to delight in the smallest glimmer reflecting back at them from the universe.

Let your love shine like a lighthouse in the storm.

Let love be the name you answer to.

Know that you are loved, my friend.

I'm *so* glad you were born.

[illegible]

# APPENDIX

# Appendix

## ADDITIONAL RESOURCES

### CRISIS AND SUPPORT RESOURCES (within the U.S.)

**Suicide and Crisis Lifeline**
**Call: 988**
**988lifeline.org**
24/7 support in English and Spanish

---

**Alcoholics Anonymous**
**www.aa.org**
Find meetings, connect with support services in your area, and access other resources and literature.

---

**Narcotics Anonymous**
**www.na.org**
Find meetings, connect with support services in your area, and access other resources and literature.

**SAMHSA (Substance Abuse & Mental Health Services Admin.)**
**Call: 1-800-662-4357**
**www.samhsa.gov**
Free, confidential, 24/7, 365-day-a-year treatment referral and information service (in English and Spanish) for individuals and families facing mental and/or substance use disorders.

---

**National Domestic Violence Hotline**
**1-800-799-7233**
**www.thehotline.org/get-help/**
24/7 free, confidential support, call or chat

---

**U.S. Toll-Free # for Canadian Suicide Prevention Hotline**
**1-877-330-6366**

---

**The Trevor Project**
**www.thetrevorproject.org/get-help/**
Connect to a crisis counselor 24/7, 365 days a year, from anywhere in the U.S via text, chat, or phone. Free and confidential support, suicide-prevention, and resources for LGBTQ+ youth.

---

## QUICK REFERENCE

**The Love Languages according to Gary Chapman:**

- Words of Affirmation
- Quality Time
- Acts of Service
- Receiving Gifts

**Signs of Narcissistic Personality Disorder:**

- Lack of empathy
- Excessive need for admiration
- Grandiose sense of self/Self-importance
- Interpersonally exploitive behavior/Manipulative
- Sense of entitlement
- Arrogant behavior or attitude
- Attention-seeking
- Arrogance
- Fantasies of greatness / Preoccupation with power, physical attractiveness, success

**The Twelve Steps of Alcoholics Anonymous:**

1. We admitted we were powerless over alcohol — that our lives had become unmanageable.
2. Came to believe that a Power greater than ourselves could restore us to sanity.
3. Made a decision to turn our will and our lives over to the care of God as we understood Him.
4. Made a searching and fearless moral inventory of ourselves.
5. Admitted to God, to ourselves, and to another human being the exact nature of our wrongs.
6. Were entirely ready to have God remove all these defects of character.
7. Humbly asked Him to remove our shortcomings.
8. Made a list of all persons we had harmed, and became willing to make amends to them all.
9. Made direct amends to such people wherever possible, except when to do so would injure them or others.
10. Continued to take personal inventory and when we were wrong promptly admitted it.

11. Sought through prayer and meditation to improve our conscious contact with God as we understood Him, praying only for knowledge of His will for us and the power to carry that out.
12. Having had a spiritual awakening as the result of these Steps, we tried to carry this message to alcoholics, and to practice these principles in all our affairs.

# ACKNOWLEDGMENTS

This book is a love letter. It is a book about restoring faith in ourselves and our fellow humans and finding our way on the messy road of life. I could not have written it without every single human (and quite a few beloved fur-friends) along my life's journey. Every harsh word, every kind gesture, every lesson learned, every setback, and every hand outstretched in community shaped my understanding not only of how the world hurts but also how it heals.

I thank my dear friend, Kelly, who encouraged the idea when it was still only a dream, my husband, Alan, who has helped me grow and learn and love over these many decades, and my children (biological and bonus) who helped me see so clearly the power and grace of unconditional love.

To my friends, my family, and the communities I've been a part of: thank you! I love you all.

# ABOUT THE AUTHOR

Cheri Allan is a human author alive on this swirling globe of amazement.

She also writes humorous contemporary romance which is, coincidentally, about love.

Find her on various social media and her website.
www.cheriallan.com

www.ingramcontent.com/pod-product-compliance
Lightning Source LLC
Chambersburg PA
CBHW070759280326
41934CB00012B/2978
* 9 7 8 0 9 9 6 8 9 5 5 3 8 *